Surviving the Squeeze

C0-AKE-072

Also by Stephen M. Pollan and Mark Levine

The Total Negotiator

The Big Fix-Up: Renovating Your Home Without Losing Your Shirt

The Business of Living

Your Recession Handbook: How to Thrive and Profit During Hard Times

The Field Guide to Starting a Business

The Field Guide to Home Buying in America

Surviving the Squeeze

The Baby Boomer's Guide to
Financial Well-Being
in the 1990s

Stephen M. Pollan and Mark Levine

Collier Books
Macmillan Publishing Company
New York

Maxwell Macmillan Canada
Toronto

Maxwell Macmillan International
New York Oxford Singapore Sydney

Copyright © 1994 by Stephen M. Pollan and Mark Levine
All rights reserved. No part of this book may be reproduced or transmitted in any
form or by any means, electronic or mechanical, including photocopying, recording,
or by any information storage and retrieval system, without permission in writing
from the Publisher.

Collier Books

Macmillan Publishing Company

866 Third Avenue

New York, NY 10022

Maxwell Macmillan Canada, Inc.

1200 Eglinton Avenue East

Suite 200

Don Mills, Ontario M3C 3N1

Macmillan Publishing Company is part of the Maxwell Communication Group of
Companies.

The "Money-Attitude Analysis" on pages 28–29 is reprinted with permission
from Melvin Prince.

The chart on p. 171 of "Annual Costs" of raising a child is © *American
Demographics* (August 1991), and is reprinted with permission; for subscription
information please call (800) 828-1133.

The table on pages 192–93 projecting the cost of a college education is taken
from *The Financial Planning Guide to the 1990s*, by Gary L. Klott, copyright © 1990
Gary Klott, and is reprinted by permission of Times Books, a division of Random
House, Inc.

Library of Congress Cataloging-in-Publication Data

Pollan, Stephen M.
    Surviving the squeeze: the baby boomer's guide to financial well-being in the
1990s/Stephen M. Pollan and Mark Levine. — 1st Collier Books ed.
        p.   cm.
    Includes index.
    ISBN 0-02-081168-3
    1. Baby boom generation—Finance, Personal. 2. Financial security. I. Levine,
Mark. II. Title.
HG179.P55544   1994
332.024—dc20   93-41931

Macmillan books are available at special discounts for bulk purchases for sales
promotions, premiums, fund-raising, or educational use. For details, contact:

Special Sales Director
Macmillan Publishing Company
866 Third Avenue
New York, NY 10022

10 9 8 7 6 5 4 3 2 1

Printed in the United States of America

The authors dedicate this book to the late Gregor Roy: poet, teacher, actor, and—above all—friend.

Contents

Preface

My picture on the jacket of this book gives me away: I'm not a baby boomer. But that doesn't mean I'm not intimately aware of what it's like to be part of America's largest generation. For the past fifteen years of my private practice as a financial and legal adviser, the overwhelming majority of my clients have been baby boomers. Due to the deeply personal nature of the counseling I provide, I've been involved not only with the facts of their lives but with their dreams and fears as well. My legal partner is a baby boomer, and so is my coauthor. I'm also the father of four boomers.

In my private practice and writing, I've advised baby boomers about many things, including how and when to borrow money; how to buy, sell, and renovate real estate; how to start their own businesses; how to ask for raises; and of late, unfortunately, how to negotiate severance pay. I like to think I've been successful at it. I believe one of the reasons for my success is that I empathize with my clients' problems. I put myself in their shoes and treat their problems as my own. Perhaps that's why for the past five years or so, I've been as dismayed as my baby boomer clients.

It was just during these past few years that the fix baby boomers found themselves in was becoming clear: Parents were getting older; children were arriving on the scene; hair was starting to thin and go gray; and jobs were starting to vanish. It's a dilemma I call "the squeeze": possible bills for both elder care and college tuition coming due when boomers should begin saving for their own retirement and are finding their streams of income under threat. My clients were convinced that since they didn't have the financial resources to meet all these obligations, they were failures—or had been poor money managers. I knew that couldn't be the case, so I began looking for answers.

Preface

When I first looked at the squeeze, my ideas were similar to those you'd find in any good financial magazine or hear from a traditional financial adviser. I looked at the potential bills, checked when they'd come due, and tried to figure out how my clients could come up with the money in time. But the longer I studied the squeeze and the more I examined the traditional advice being offered, the clearer it became that the traditional answers wouldn't work. How could I ask someone who's barely making ends meet now and who's worried about her job to start saving 25 percent of her income? The traditional advice was logical, but it wasn't practical. My clients couldn't be viewed as failures for not being able to do the impossible. Since I spend my time advising real people, I needed to offer solutions they could actually use.

That search is what led me to the somewhat unconventional program you'll find in this book. I began with only two prerequisites: first, that the program work; and second, that it actually could be put in place not only by saints and misers but by real baby boomers. I believe I've found an answer, a way to survive the squeeze. Moreover, in the process, I think I've stumbled on to something even more important: a blueprint for actually getting more out of life. The advice you'll read in this book has worked for my clients. I believe it can work for you, too.

—STEPHEN M. POLLAN

Acknowledgments

We would like to thank the following experts, authors, scholars, seers, pundits, and thinkers for all their help: Gary Ambrose, William Archey, Ruth Beltran, Leonard Berry, Judith Briles, Arnold Brown, David Campbell, Sally Carr, Anthony Casale, William Charland, Gerrie Charnow, Bob Dillon, Ethel Drayton-Craig, John Duffy, Mark Edmundson, James Freund, Valerie Friedman, Susan Garbrecht, Andrew Garvin, Mary Giannini, Herb Goldberg, Ross Goldstein, Bruce Greenwald, Shelley Greenwald, Lisa Steinhowser Hackle, Neil Howe, Carole Hyatt, Landon Jones, Jack Kaye, Dale Klamfoth, Erik Kobell, Emily Koltnow, Priscilla Ann LaBarbera, Ira Landess, Howard Leifman, Paul Leinberger, Frank Lichtenberg, Paul Charles Light, Charles Logue, Frank Loscalzo, Olivia Mellan, Cheryl Merser, Mitchell Moss, Katherine Newman, Dan O'Brien, Faith Popcorn, Mel Prince, Marilyn Puder-York, Jane Purcell, Tom Rodman, Deborah Shah, Carter Smith, Charles Sodikoff, Donald Snider, William Starbuck, Michael Stone, Peter Strauss, William Strauss, Arthur Taylor, Joel Tucciarone, David Wallechinsky, Ian Wilcox, Marilynn Williamson, Martin Yate, and Christopher York.

On a more personal note, we would like to thank Shannon Carney, Natalie Chapman, Debbie Harkins, Gabrielle Kleinman, Stuart Krichevsky, and Jane Morrow, without whose encouragement, support, inspiration, comments, and help we could not have written this book.

Finally, we would most of all like to thank our wives, Corky Pollan and Deirdre Martin Levine, for their advice, patience, and understanding.

Surviving the Squeeze

Chapter One

The Big Squeeze

The baby boom generation may never achieve the relative economic success of the generations immediately preceding it or following it.

—the 1980 U.S. budget

The baby boom generation is the engine that drives America.

That's because the 76 million people born between 1946 and 1964 represent about one-third of this nation's population.

Boomers' tastes are the national tastes. Blue jeans and T-shirts are the national uniform, and rock and roll is the national music because that's what boomers wear and listen to.

Boomer morality is the national morality. The tolerance individual baby boomers generally have for those who look, think, act, believe, speak, and live differently is leading this nation toward addressing and overcoming societal divisions.

The mood of the baby boom generation is the national mood. In the 1960s, boomers were rebellious and angry, and the nation shook on its foundations. In the 1970s, boomers were introspective and apathetic, and the nation simultaneously turned inward and off. In the 1980s, boomers were overconfident, and the nation built an economic boom out of thin air. Now, in the 1990s, boomers are fearful, and the nation lives under a black cloud.

The Big Squeeze

In late 1991, a couple came to see me for some financial advice. Sydney and Lucy Carton* had called me on the recommendation of Lucy's friend, whom I had helped buy a home earlier in the year. As we sat down at the round table in my office, I asked Sydney and Lucy to tell me about themselves.

They own a two-bedroom apartment on the Upper West Side of Manhattan. Sydney is forty-five, and works as an account executive at a midsized advertising agency. Lucy is forty-three and is an editor of a major national magazine. They have one child, an eight-year-old daughter named Brittany. All three are in good health.

After some small talk about how precocious eight-year-olds can be, I asked Sydney and Lucy what I could do for them. They were silent. That didn't surprise me; it happens a lot. I told them not to worry and instead asked them to tell me about their fears. It was as if a verbal dam had broken.

"I don't think I'm going to be able to pay for Brittany's college education," Sydney admitted.

"My mother's getting older," Lucy added. "She's not that well off, and I'm afraid she's going to turn to us for help. And I don't know how we're going to come up with the money."

"I'm forty-five," Sydney confessed, "and I haven't saved a penny for retirement yet. With day care and the mortgage payments, it's been tough, and now we've got to start worrying about college and Lucy's mom. I don't see how I'll ever be able to put enough money away for us to retire."

"And to make matters worse," Lucy interjected, "there have been lots of rumors at the magazine. I think they're going to start laying people off. I don't know what we'll do if I'm let go," she admitted.

"Yeah," added Sydney forlornly. "We can't make it on just my salary." The two looked at each other and then turned to

---

*Not their real names. Throughout this book, I've changed the names of my clients to protect their privacy.

face me. "It's like we're in one of those old horror movies," Sydney said. "We're trapped in a room where the walls, floor, and ceiling are closing in on us. There's no escape."

Sydney and Lucy may have felt alone in their anxiety, but their story was becoming increasingly familiar. They had a right to feel trapped, frightened, and frustrated. Many, if not most, of my baby boomer clients had similar problems and fears. I explained to Sydney and Lucy that the situation they found themselves in wasn't their fault. They weren't paying for mistakes or past selfishness. Nor were they powerless victims. They had the intelligence and resources to pull themselves out of their current troubles, to take charge of their lives. And I pledged to show them how.

Later that day, after Sydney and Lucy had left, I jotted down some notes about how widespread their problem was. Those notes were the seed of this book.

Nearly every week a baby boomer client comes to my office for a consultation. And while each individual's circumstances are unique, the fears expressed are remarkably the same.

- They're afraid they won't be able to pay for their offspring's college educations.
- They're fearful that aging parents will need financial help—which they'll have a difficult time providing.
- They see no possibility of ever being able to save for their own retirements.
- And they're uncertain of their jobs—if they still have them.

As a baby boomer, you don't need me to tell you that these fears are real and justifiable. Let's take a look at them one by one.

How Will You Pay for Your Child's College Education?

A higher percentage of baby boomers went to college than any previous generation. That's partly because many were brought up in home environments that stressed generational advance-

What Was the Baby Boom and Why Did It Happen?

The baby boom was the nineteen-year period between 1946 and 1964 when approximately 76 million babies were born in the United States. The surge in births was a demographic phenomenon, since the number of babies born both before and after this period was much smaller. The only other countries that experienced anything like this surge in births were Canada, Australia, and New Zealand. The peak year of the American baby boom was 1957, when about 4.3 million children were born. That remains the single highest number of births in any one year in American history.

While the reasons for the baby boom are still being debated, most demographers and historians believe it was due to the postwar prosperity and hopefulness felt in the world's four young, expansive, democratic nations. The optimistic spirit and economic boom of the times led young people to marry and begin having children earlier than previous generations. At the same time, older couples, who delayed having children due to World War II, began reproducing. The birthrate remained high because continued economic prosperity led those young couples to keep on having more children. In effect, a small generation spawned a large generation by beginning to reproduce earlier and then continuing to reproduce over a longer period of time than ever before

Are Boomers All Alike?

Because they represented a demographic anomaly, baby boomers have always been treated as a monolithic group. Nothing could be further from the truth. Due to their size, boomers are a very diverse group. They do, however, all share some things—besides common birth dates. Boomers grew up being crowded. They were born in crowded hospitals, went to crowded schools, and played in crowded playgrounds and parks. That crowding led to unprecedented competition for places in college, jobs, and homes. Boomers also share a sense of bittersweet history. The promise of Camelot and civil rights turned into the assassinations of JFK, Martin Luther King, Jr., RFK, and Malcom X. The Peace Corps and the Alliance for Progress were transformed into Vietnam. Woodstock became Altamont. Boomers were told the world was at their feet but were taught to duck under their desks in case of nuclear attack.

Boomer Versus Boomer

The best way to demonstrate that baby boomers aren't a monolithic group economically is to look at the differences in circumstances between older and younger baby boomers. Older boomers had the first crack at job openings and promotions and were able to buy into the soaring real estate market early on. Younger boomers have therefore had a harder time finding jobs and advancing in their careers and were forced to either forgo buying a home or buy when the market was at its peak and then see it collapse. All this has led to younger boomers being less well off than their older siblings. But the tide may be turning. Younger boomers are generally, like most younger siblings in families, more self-sufficient and better adjusted. Others' expectations of them, and their expectations of themselves, were never as high as those of and about their older siblings. That means they may have a much easier time abandoning outmoded assumptions and therefore surviving the squeeze.

ment: Each generation was supposed to do better and achieve more than the previous one. Parents who never attended college pushed for their kids to go to a university. And those parents who went to the local city or state college tried to send their kids to private schools.

I can see this clearly in my own family. My parents never went to college but impressed on me the importance of my getting an education. I went to the City University of New York. When it came time for my children to go to college, I wanted them to get an even better education than I did, and so they went to private universities.

While this was a wonderful idea, it has led to trouble for many baby boomers. The educational success of the baby boom generation has devalued the college diploma. It's a simple matter of supply and demand: With so many college graduates around, the value of a sheepskin diminished. In today's job market, college degrees are just about the equivalent of what high school diplomas were in the 1950s. This has led many boomers to feel that their children simply must get a degree if they're going to make it.

Reared on this notion of generational advancement, many boomers feel they must provide more for their kids than their parents did for them. That means if a boomer didn't go to college, his child must; if he went to a state university, his child must go to a private college; if the boomer went to a private college, his child must go to an Ivy League school; and if he went to an Ivy League school, his kids must go on to law school or medical school.

That's how Sydney Carton felt. His parents were, like me, graduates of the City University of New York. Sydney was encouraged to excel at school, and when it came time to attend college, he applied to both Ivy League and state universities. He ended up going to the State University of New York at Binghamton—a fine institution consistently ranked among the best colleges for the money in America by *Money*. But seeing that there's something of an old-boy network in his industry— alumni of Ivy League colleges recruiting recent graduates from

6

their own schools and easing their climb up the corporate ladder—Sydney has sworn to give his daughter that advantage.

Putting aside the questionable logic of such an attitude for a moment, let's look at two economic facts of life:

First, boomers who want to pay for their child's college tuition are taking on a bill their parents didn't. Record numbers of baby boomers were able to afford college not because their parents' generation footed the bill—either directly or through government scholarships—but because, in general, they took out loans. Sure, many moms and dads contributed what they could, and some did actually foot the bill, but on the whole, boomers borrowed the money themselves. (Sydney took out student loans to go to SUNY Binghamton.) Now, because many have bought into this idea of generational advancement, boomers are trying to pay for their kids' tuition out of their own pockets.

And second, college tuition fees are growing at a much faster rate than baby boomer incomes and at an extraordinarily faster rate than baby boomer savings—if the boomer in question has any savings at all. (Sydney and Lucy's combined income simply has not, and will not, keep pace with the rising cost of an Ivy League education for their daughter.) In the year 2001, tuition at a public college will be about $9,500 annually, for a four-year total of around $38,000. Tuition at a private college in 2001 will be around $25,500 per year, for a four-year total of about $102,000.

To make matters worse, that's not the only huge bill Sydney and Lucy, or you, may be facing.

How Will You Take Care of Your Aging Parent(s)?

Thanks to medical advances, increased attention to nutrition, and an overall societal concern with physical health, the parents of the baby boom generation will be around much longer than they anticipated. That means they'll be able to impart their wisdom to grandchildren and take pleasure in a long, rich life. But it also means the odds are greatly increased that they'll

have extraordinarily large health-care bills in the final years of
their lives.

Anywhere from 30 to 60 percent of those who are now between sixty and sixty-five will need some type of long-term
health-care services. And the figures go up for each five-year
age group. By age seventy-five one in three people will need
long-term care; and by eighty-five the figure is one out of two.

If aging parents don't account for increased longevity in
their financial planning, it's possible they could run out of
money. Even those who may have sufficient assets in their estates may not wish to tap their investment principal. Some
well-off elderly may be too wrapped up in their fears to realize
the extent of their financial resources. Whatever the case, many
boomers who grew up being told that their parents were sacri-
ficing for them and who saw their parents help their grandparents feel driven to provide for parents in their time of perceived
need.

That's how Lucy felt. An only child, Lucy grew up in a
middle-class suburb outside Boston. When Lucy's maternal
grandmother was widowed, Lucy's parents immediately took
her into their home. "Nana" became part of the household.
Lucy's mother always told stories about how Nana had strug-
gled to provide for the kids during the war years while "Pop"
was over in Europe. While it was never stated, there was an assumed quid pro quo: In return for those sacrifices, Lucy's mother cared for her mother for as long as she lived. Now, years later,
Lucy's mother was widowed. And the unstated family assumption suddenly resurfaced: Lucy's mother hinted that she'd like
to move in. And Lucy felt obligated to take her in and support
her if she needed financial help.

The cost of such parental support could be substantial.
Nursing-home care currently costs anywhere from $25,000 to
$70,000 per year, depending on the level of care and the quali-
ty of the facility, with the average falling around $31,000. If we
assume that care increases at a rate of 4 percent a year, between
now and 2001 the average annual cost for nursing-home care

will then be about $43,000. (In-home custodial care is less expensive—about $100 per visit by a registered nurse and $10–$15 per hour for a home aide—but over time it still represents a substantial cost.)

That's a frightening figure on its own. But when you add the fact that some boomers will have a child in college and a parent in a nursing home simultaneously, the numbers become horrifying. (When Lucy and Sydney's daughter, Brittany, becomes eighteen and in her first year of college, Lucy's mother will be seventy-five.)

At present, there are close to 4 million men and women with children under fifteen who are also caring for a parent—that's more than 7 percent of parents with children of that age. As we move closer to the turn of the century, the percentage will certainly increase. In 2001, the combined bill for a year in a private college and a year in a nursing home will be $68,500.

If you're planning to save for that eventuality, you should have started yesterday, and you're certainly not going to have much money left for your own tomorrow.

How Will You Prepare for Your Own Retirement?

While most baby boomers are trying to prepare for retirement, generally they don't have enough, or at least as much as they would like. And the majority of the savings they do have is locked into company pension plans that are, in most cases, underfunded and at risk from management mistakes. While some pundits have cited this as a generational character flaw, it is actually quite understandable.

More boomers than in previous generations chose to live on their own as singles. In 1904 the average age of men when they left their parents' home was twenty-four; in 1970 it was nineteen. That meant they had greater expenses than those who stayed home until marriage. In addition, unlike previous generations, a substantial number of boomers began their working lives with a built-in budget deficit: their student loans.

It was next to impossible for most baby boomers to put a dent in this deficit, since incomes simply didn't grow fast enough to keep up with expenses. Whereas their parents' incomes increased 524 percent in real terms between the ages of twenty and thirty, baby boomers' incomes increased only 34 percent between the ages of twenty and thirty. That's because all those boomers competing for jobs kept salaries low. In fact, while the average American's wages rose continuously for twenty-six years after World War II, wages stopped rising, in real terms, in 1973, just as boomers started to flood the job market. Adjusting for inflation, the average boomer is making no more money today than he or she was earning in 1973.

While incomes stagnated, real estate prices soared. All those boomers competing for a finite number of properties pushed values up. That made it more difficult for boomers to buy homes and thereby shield their income from taxes while taking advantage of inflation, as their parents had done. Although this real-estate boom helped many parents of baby boomers establish estates, it also led to a cruel irony: Most baby boomers cannot afford to buy homes in the towns they grew up in.

Boomers have also been forced to do without many of the government support programs that helped their parents. The ability of the previous generation to save and create wealth was based, to a large extent, on the support provided by government programs like Social Security, the GI Bill, and FHA mortgages. In effect, government removed some of the strain on the prior generation's stream of income. Now, however, the bills for all this governmental support are coming due in the form of the budget deficit. And since your parents will decapitate any politician who threatens to cut or tax entitlement, you'll be handed the bill—unless you, too, pass it on to your kids.

Despite these built-in disadvantages, many boomers tried to replicate, and even surpass, their parents' standard of living. After all, they were supposed to do better than the previous generation; from the moment of their birth baby boomers were proclaimed by their parents and the nation as the best and brightest.

Many boomers have kept, and continue to keep, the illusion of generational advancement alive by making sacrifices. More boomers remain single than in previous generations. Those who do marry do so later than their parents, and most form two-income households. Boomers spend more of their monthly income on shelter than previous generations, and those who own their own homes carry a much bigger mortgage debt. More boomers are remaining childless than previous generations. And those who do choose parenthood are having fewer children and at a later age.

Even with these dramatic sacrifices, the majority of baby boomers simply didn't have enough money to maintain the lifestyle they, their parents, and society expected of them. That has led many to go into debt. Consumer debt increased from $1.3 trillion in 1980 to $3.4 trillion in 1990. Out of the 96 million American households, 85 million owed money at some point in 1990. The main source of this surge in borrowing seems to be the widening use of credit cards to make everyday purchases. Now, as they reach middle age—the time when previous generations could make up for the youthful inability to save—boomers are overleveraged and are facing those gigantic bills for college tuition and nursing-home care.

That's the situation Sydney and Lucy found themselves in. Both took out substantial student loans to go to college. After graduating, they each got their own apartment. They focused on their individual careers at first rather than looking to get married. And while both are relatively successful in their chosen fields, their incomes haven't kept up with costs. When they did decide to marry, they were in their mid-thirties. Once they were married, they looked to buy a home in the suburbs near where Sydney grew up. But although their combined income was twice what Sydney's father was earning when his parents bought a home in the area, they just couldn't afford to buy there. Instead, they bought an apartment in the city. Still, the mortgage payment represented a substantial share of their combined monthly income. They began furnishing their apartment while continuing to try to maintain the middle-class life-styles they enjoyed when they were growing up. The only way they could do that was by putting most of their purchases on credit cards. Now they're in debt, have little savings for their own retirements, and are facing gigantic college-tuition bills for their daughter and elder-care bills for Lucy's mother, both of which will be due when Sydney and Lucy are in their late fifties.

And if the scenario facing Sydney, Lucy, and other baby boomers, like you, wasn't dreadful enough, your incomes—the only tools around to help overcome all these obstacles—are no longer safe.

Your Stream of Income Is Threatened

Most boomers grew up thinking they'd be rewarded for doing what they were supposed to do; that they were entitled to success whether it was at home, in school, or on the job. It's easy to see where this attitude came from.

Baby boomers were born at a time of economic prosperity. Most Americans were doing better than they ever had before—in fact, better than they'd ever expected to do. It was the time of the great migration of families from crowded cities into idyllic suburbs. Many of the parents of boomers felt a bit guilty about their prosperity, having been brought up during the Great Depression and World War II.

One way they could spend and consume without guilt was to say they "were doing it for the kids." Whether buying a house with a lawn and a basketball hoop, a station wagon with wood panels on the side, or a color television, everything was done "for the kids." After singing this refrain for years and years, many boomers began to assume they were entitled to such spending. Why? Because they were the best and the brightest, of course.

Just as their parents were superficially dedicating themselves to boomer gratification, so, too, was the mass culture. The birth of the baby boom coincided with the media explosion. All the new newspapers, magazines, radio shows, and

The Baby Bust Generation

Even as the baby boom generation begins facing its great challenge—the big squeeze—demographers, social scientists, and marketers are beginning to shift their focus to the 45 million Americans who make up the next generation. Not surprising when you realize that these individuals are just turning twenty-five—a prime spending and consuming age. While there's no consensus yet on what to call these twentysomethings (Generation X, Thirteeners, and Slackers are among the most popular choices), one thing's for certain. They won't have much in common with baby boomers. They are the first generation that grew up primarily in dual-career families, 50 percent of which experienced divorce. With all the boomers still in the work force, they have few apparent job opportunities. Many feel they'll have to pay the bills for the previous two generations' excesses.

television programs needed something to write and talk about. Why not the baby boom generation? They were, after all, a phenomenon.

It wasn't long before advertisers and marketers realized that boomers—who as a group make up one-third of the population—represented an unprecedented customer base. At first, boomers were targeted through their parents, then on their own, and now through their children. For the first time in history products were created to satisfy young people's tastes. With their parents, the media, and industry all catering to their needs and wants, is it any wonder the baby boom began to feel entitled to such attention?

Once boomers entered the job market, many expected they'd be catered to just as they were at home and at school. If they showed up at work and did their job, they'd have a position and would receive steady raises. And for a while things worked out that way. Across America the work force, particularly middle management, expanded dramatically to absorb all those boomers. The baby boom generation's feeling of entitlement fit in well with the concept of corporate paternalism (the company as benevolent parent) that had been around since the beginning of the industrial age. While the boomers didn't, in real terms, earn as much as their parents, they did have secure jobs and did receive steady raises and promotions.

The last bastion of corporate paternalism crumbled on February 24, 1993, when IBM, the corporation that had made lifetime employment the core of its culture, announced it would be laying off employees. These layoffs confirmed what pundits had been saying since the late 1980s: Job security and the corporate ladder were gone.

Throughout the recession of the late 1980s, business leaders of both large and small companies spoke of the need to thin ranks in order to survive. But as the recession lingered, many business pundits began to preach about the need to completely overhaul the corporate structure.

Temporary layoffs of blue-collar workers turned into permanent termination of white-collar workers. Entire departments and layers of management were eliminated in the desire to streamline bureaucracies. For the first time, many of those boomers in middle management either were given pink slips themselves or saw peers get them. And since every business was going through the same dramatic process, new jobs were tough to find. Employers now speak of project, rather than lifetime, employment. And boomers now know they have no job security.

Without savings to draw upon, with huge bills for college tuition and parental nursing-home care looming in the future and with no secure stream of income to draw upon, is it any wonder Sydney and Lucy, and you, feel trapped and frightened?

The Big Squeeze Is a Unique Dilemma

Even when these facts are laid out plainly, there are many, including some of my peers in financial-counseling circles, who refuse to feel any sympathy for baby boomers. These people say every generation has had to cope with such dilemmas and that this is just one more example of baby boomer self-absorption. While middle age *is* traditionally the time when responsibilities fall on a generation, I believe the problem of the baby boom is unique.

First, no generation in American history has ever had such poor timing. Because they married later and had children later and because their parents are living longer, boomers are the first Americans to face college tuition and elder-care bills at the same time as they would normally begin saving for retirement. Their parents generally faced these bills one at a time: first college tuition; then retirement savings; and finally, if the grandparents were unusually long lived, elder care.

Second, few generations in American history have ever had such bad luck financially. The baby boomer generation is facing unprecedented bills at a time when they have no savings, their streams of income are, at best, threatened, and the global economy is in the doldrums. Sure, the Great Depression was a lot worse, but at least that was temporary. The current economic restructuring looks as if it won't be completed for decades.

And third, no generation in American history has ever faced such a huge gap between expectations and reality. While middle age has always been a time when youthful dreams gave way to grown-up reality, the shock has been more dramatic for boomers. That's because no generation ever had such high expectations. The baby boomers were expected to surpass their parents economically and lead the nation into an era of affluence. Instead, it's destined to be the first American generation to do worse than its predecessor economically, and it appears likely it will preside over a period of, at best, economic stagnation.

Anger, bitterness, frustration, and assigning blame will not help you secure your stream of income, educate your children, care for your parents, provide for your retirement, or achieve some degree of personal peace. All these feelings, however justifiable, only lead down into a never-ending abyss of self-pity and despair. Just as a mourner must move from denial to anger to acceptance, so, too, must the baby boom generation come to terms with its shattered expectations.

Surviving the Squeeze

One of life's great lessons—one that, it seems, can only be learned in middle age—is that no one is entitled to success. We are all at the mercy of larger forces over which we have little control. Life serves its own purposes and is its own reward. It's as if we are all participants in a cosmic poker game. You have been dealt a hand. Neither you nor anyone else had control over the cards. All you can do is play the cards the best you can. That's not a passive philosophy, it's a realistic one. Success and failure aren't quantifiable. Failure is giving up. Success is doing the best you can with the resources you have. In the cosmic poker game, the winner isn't the one with the most chips at the end but the one who has done the most with the chips available.

There's no shortage of advice out there purporting to tell you how to get the most out of your chips. In every bookstore, in most magazines and newspapers, and on countless radio and television programs, you can find tips on how to pay for your child's college education, how to take care of your aging parents, how to save for retirement, and how to move up the corporate ladder. Almost all this advice is well meaning and based on sound financial calculations.

It doesn't take a financial whiz to offer this advice, to figure out how much someone needs to put aside to pay for things like college tuition, elder care, or retirement. Let's go through a typical financial-planning session.

Say Sydney and Lucy were referred to a financial adviser who takes a more traditional approach than I do. The first thing the adviser—let's call her Deborah—would ask Sydney and Lucy is what their most important goal was. If push came to shove, they'd probably say paying for Brittany's college education was their most important goal. Deborah would ask how old Brittany was. She would then punch up on her computer the projected cost of tuition the year Brittany will turn eighteen. Deborah then calculates how many years Sydney and Lucy have before the bill comes due. Believe it or not, that finishes the tough part of the financial planning.

If Sydney and Lucy needed to come up with a great deal of money in a short period of time, Deborah would tell them to save and invest a substantial part of their income (probably 25 percent) in a financial instrument that, while risky, will pay a substantial return quickly—probably a stock portfolio. But since Sydney and Lucy have ten years to work with, Deborah would advise them to invest in a plan with a lower, but more certain, return—probably a series of zero coupon bonds that come due the years Brittany turns eighteen, nineteen, twenty, and twenty-one and pay just about the amount her college tuition will cost. She would tell Sydney and Lucy what such a bond would cost, and Sydney and Lucy would nod and write the figure down.

Having finished with the first problem—Brittany's college tuition—Deborah would then ask Sydney and Lucy about their second problem. Lucy would immediately bring up her mother, and Sydney, not wanting to appear selfish, would agree. Deborah would then go through the exact same process again, except this time factoring in the cost of elder care and the approximate time when the bills would again be coming due. Since the number here wouldn't be as firm as the figure for college tuition, Deborah would probably recommend that Sydney and Lucy put a set percentage of their income into an investment instrument. Sydney and Lucy would once again nod and write the figure down.

Deborah, happy at how well things were going, would then ask about Sydney and Lucy's retirement plans. Embarrassed, Sydney and Lucy would admit they had nothing other than the 401K plans offered by their employers. Deborah would give them a quick lecture on the need to provide for their own retirement and once again go through the same process. This time she would set as a goal their being able to retire at age sixty five and maintain their current life-style until age eighty-five. Deborah would determine how much that would take, figure how long Sydney and Lucy had to come up with the money, and then recommend how much of their income they should invest where. Once again, Sydney and Lucy would nod and write the information down.

Satisfied with a fine day's work, Deborah would congratulate Sydney and Lucy for taking charge of their own lives, shake their hands, and wish them well. Sydney and Lucy would get home, look at their notes, and not know whether to laugh or cry.

The Traditional Approach Won't Work

This approach to financial planning has worked for many years and remains the mainstay of most media and private advisers. There's only one problem with it: It won't work for most baby boomers.

First, many boomers have barely enough income to cover their expenses and the interest on their debts. It's difficult for them to save anything, let alone a sizable portion of their income. My average client is happy to just break even. To put aside such sizable sums would require a complete and instantaneous overhaul of their financial attitudes and a radical shift in their life-styles. Such steps may make sense as long-term goals, but they aren't short-term solutions to immediate problems.

Second, many boomers have streams of income that are shaky at best. Asking a boomer with a secure job and future to set aside 10 percent of his income is one thing. Asking that of someone who may not have a job tomorrow or who may have just taken a 20 percent pay cut in order to get back in the job market, is something else entirely.

And third, many boomers have more than one of these huge expenses coming due at the same time. While unlikely, it's not impossible for a boomer to save, say, 10 percent of her income for her child's college tuition or 15 percent of her income for elder care or even 20 percent of her income for retirement. But I believe it *is* impossible for her to do all three at once.

Slowly but surely many boomers are realizing that there is no way they can follow traditional financial advice. In response, some turn to high-yield, high-risk investments in an effort to get rich quick. Sometimes the gambles work, but more often than not they end in disaster. Other boomers are going even deeper into debt, refinancing their homes in order to pick up some much-needed cash. Of course, that just adds one more monthly drain on an already tight and endangered stream of income. Still others are trying to set up priorities for the demands on them, weighing the future against their current quality of life and then choosing between their child's education, their parent's well-being, and their own future. I don't think anyone other than Solomon could be comfortable making such decisions.

If the traditional approach doesn't work and the alternatives are all bad, what's left?

The New Approach Is to Throw Out Faulty Assumptions

That's one of the first questions I'm asked by most of my new clients. Generally, clients like Sydney and Lucy come to me because they're at a loss for what to do. Sydney and Lucy, like most of my baby boomer clients, came expecting either the same traditional advice they know won't work or a sales pitch for some esoteric, get-rich-quick investment scheme. I gave them neither. What I suggested to Sydney and Lucy, and what I'm suggesting to you, is that baby boomers need to take an entirely new approach to personal financial planning. You need to throw out all the assumptions you've been basing your financial lives on.

What assumptions am I talking about? The first is that a child must go to college and that if she does the parent must pay the tuition bill. The second is that aging parents won't have enough money to live on if they get ill and if they don't a child must pick up the tab. The third is that everyone must stop working at age sixty-five. And the fourth is that saving money is the best financial-planning device.

I suggest discarding all these assumptions not only because they are leading to tremendous frustration and anxiety but because I believe each and every one of them is wrong for the baby boomer. I don't believe every child of a baby boomer should go to college or that if they do the boomer should pay the tuition bill. I don't believe most of the aging parents of baby boomers need financial assistance or that if they do it must come from the boomer. I believe that for the baby boom generation, retirement is a nonevent. And I believe saving money is the *least* effective financial-planning device.

I'll get into each of these new hypotheses in detail in subsequent chapters, but before you throw this book across the room, let me explain each just briefly.

Must Your Child Go to College (and Should You Pay for It)?

College has never been right for everyone. That's why half of all college students drop out. I tell my boomer clients that while college is an option, it's not the only option. There are many excellent jobs that don't require college degrees. And in the next few years the nation will see a surge of interest in alternative avenues for advanced education, such as corporate-sponsored apprenticeship programs and vocational schools.

Sure, there are other reasons to get an education besides financial return. But I don't believe you need to pay upwards of $100,000 for your child to become cultured or to learn about others.

And just as there are alternatives to college, there are also alternatives to Mom and Dad paying for it. If a child decides college is the right choice for him, paying for it should be a *family* expense. That means parents and child need to form a partnership and pursue every option available. I'll be going over how to help your child decide whether college is right for him and exploring all these and other alternative methods of financing tuition in chapter 8.

Will Your Parents Need Financial Help (and Should It Come from You)?

The idea that the parents of the baby boom are one illness away from poverty is largely a myth. In fact, the silent generation, as they've been named, is collectively one of the wealthiest generations in history. But because they grew up during the Great Depression and World War II, they've always underestimated their wealth and been extremely frightened of having to repeat the deprivations of their childhood. Where will their accumulated wealth go? The bulk of it, according to most economists, will be handed over, in inheritance, to the baby boom generation. Boomers need to tell their parents to forget about leaving estates and instead take care of their own needs.

There are, of course, those aging parents who don't have the financial resources to take care of themselves. But that doesn't mean boomers should foot the bill. There's another answer: The government can help.

In chapter 7 I'll go over how to help your parents make decisions about long-term-care insurance, living trusts, durable powers of attorney for health care, living wills, prearranged and prepaid funerals, and Medicaid trusts.

Can You Afford to Retire (and Should You Even Want To)?

Among the first things most of my baby boomer clients ask me is "How will I be able to retire?" I always respond with a question of my own: "Why would you want to?" The standard notion of retirement simply doesn't fit the life or circumstances of the baby boom generation and is, in fact, dangerous.

The idea of leaving work at age sixty-five was brought to this country by FDR during the Great Depression as a way to clear some room in the job market for the masses of unemployed Americans. Society no longer needs to free up space in the work force. In fact, boomers will remain in demand as workers for years after they've reached "retirement age." That's because the generation following them is smaller and not as highly educated. Therefore, the societal need for retirement no longer exists.

And unlike previous generations, many baby boomers made a conscious and continuing effort to look for jobs and careers they found rewarding, so the personal need for retirement no longer exists. Even if a baby boomer wants to pursue the traditional pattern of retirement she'd be hard-pressed to do so, since rather than having to save for a brief period of inactivity, she needs to save for around two decades of nonworking life.

Retirement is dangerous because it turns people old before their time and because the traditional planning for it forces you to approach your life as a means to an end rather than as an end in itself.

I urge my clients to accept the idea that their goal should be to work at something they find enjoyable and rewarding for as long as they possibly can. And while they're working, they should do everything possible to ensure that if they're unable to work at some point, either due to disability, illness, or old age, they'll have a replacement for their stream of income.

Will Saving Money Really Help (and If Not, What Will)?

The best way for baby boomers to protect themselves from potential troubles isn't to save money, it's to join together with others with the same fears, form a pool, and spread out the risk. That's called insurance.

Boomers should be more concerned with their stream of income than their savings, and their goal should be to grow wealth, not simply to save money. Your stream of income is the fuel that runs your financial life. Rather than worrying about how much fuel you're stockpiling, you should be concerned with making sure your current fuel supply is secure, figuring out ways to increase fuel efficiency, and exploring ways to increase future supply. You should grow wealth because it's the only substitute for a stream of income. And wealth is created by investing, not by saving. Any risk can be minimized the same way we minimize the potential downside of other risks—by pooling our money with others.

There is hope. That's what I told Sydney and Lucy. That's what I tell all my other baby boomer clients. And that's what I'm writing this book to tell you. I've helped hundreds of baby boomers, including Sydney and Lucy, through the same frightening terrain you find yourself in. I've developed a seven-step program that enables baby boomers like you to survive the big squeeze with your nerves, assets, and families intact. And the only prerequisite is the willingness to take charge of your own financial life.

1. Rid yourself of irrational and counterproductive attitudes toward money.
2. Secure your stream of income whether you're an employee or an entrepreneur.
3. Maximize the efficiency of your stream of income by controlling your spending.
4. Insure your stream of income and your assets.
5. Help your parents take charge of their lives.
6. Help your children take charge of their financial lives.
7. Take charge of your own future by generating as much wealth as possible in order to supplement a shrinking stream of income.

While the steps may seem straightforward, the program I'll be outlining in this book is neither easy nor painless. It requires dedication, energy, and above all, courage. I know it's tough to move ahead without the comfortable baggage you've carried along for so long. Setting aside long-held beliefs and assumptions, even if they're outmoded, takes a special kind of bravery. You may feel like you're going on a journey without a map. Don't worry. I'll be serving as your guide in this uncharted terrain. I've been there before. I've helped hundreds of others overcome these same obstacles. The first step is always the hardest, but all that's really required is for you to turn this page.

Chapter Two

Money Myopia: The First Hurdle

People's money philosophies are irrational expressions of their anxieties.

—Herb Goldberg, author of Money Madness

The first step in surviving the squeeze is to rid yourself of irrational and counterproductive attitudes toward money. When I ask my baby boomer clients to abandon many of the financial assumptions they've grown up with, I invariably meet some initial resistance. It's difficult to set aside ideas on which you and your parents may have based much of your financial lives and which you may not even be aware of. Still, it's not as if I'm asking you to give up your religion or renounce your ethical principles. Yet that's how many clients react.

At first, I couldn't understand why baby boomers had such objections to my ideas. After all, here I was offering a way out of what seemed to be a hermetically sealed trap. I thought I was giving hope to the hopeless and they would jump at the opportunity to take charge of their lives. Yet my suggestions were often initially greeted with, of all things, anger. That troubled me a great deal, since in my highly personalized form of financial counseling, having a good relationship with the client is essential. I thought perhaps I wasn't making my arguments clear enough. I worried that I didn't have convincing enough evidence. I was afraid I was being glib, accusatory, condescending, or insensitive.

I decided to ask a psychotherapist-friend of mine, whose rapport with clients has always impressed me, for advice. As soon as I explained what was happening, he smiled knowingly.

Money Myopia

"You don't realize it, but you're hitting a raw nerve," he said. "It's money, not sex, that's the ultimate hot-button issue, especially for baby boomers." I always knew that money was incredibly powerful psychologically, yet I hadn't realized it was like modern-day manna, able to become whatever you want. According to psychologists, this has led money to become a blank screen onto which we can project all of our fears, attributes, and characteristics. The only other blank screen is sexuality. But for most boomers, sex doesn't have the same power as money.

That doesn't mean boomers value money over sex. It's just that, in general, boomers are more comfortable with sexuality than previous generations; it's no longer as much of a taboo as it once was. Yet money is still taboo. My psychotherapist-friend explained that he and his colleagues find people are much more willing to discuss openly their sexuality than their finances. Those clients who got angry with me felt I was violating their privacy and crossing into a taboo area.

This attitude toward money leads to a condition that I call money myopia: the inability to recognize that money has no intrinsic value and is simply a tool to be used to meet needs and achieve goals. Instead, we equate money with love, with happiness, with power, with success, maybe even with sorrow or pain, depending on our upbringing. Most of us suffer from money myopia to some degree or another.

Money Myopia Contributes to Faulty Assumptions

Why does all this matter? Because money myopia contributes to all those assumptions I outlined in the previous chapter. Part of the reason many boomers think they "must" pay for their parents' health care and their child's college education is that they falsely believe money equals love. Part of the reason many boomers feel they "must" save money is that they falsely believe money equals security. As long as money myopia remains undiagnosed, it is impossible to entirely abandon those assumptions. And if you can't abandon those assumptions, I can't help you survive the squeeze.

In addition, money myopia can keep you from implementing a rational financial program, such as the one I'll outline in the rest of this book. If your money attitudes are clouded with emotions, superstitions, and misconceptions, you won't be able to make logical decisions. You can't survive the squeeze if you prefer a savings account to a stock mutual fund because the former provides you with a bank book, while the latter offers just a piece of paper. You can't survive the squeeze if you believe the price of something is the single best indication of its value. If you can't control your own behavior regarding money, you can't take control over your financial life.

Because money attitudes are deeply held beliefs, overcoming problematic ones and curing money myopia are not a simple matter; it could take years. Unfortunately, baby boomers don't have the time.

To that end it can be extremely helpful to do a simple self-analysis, learn what your tendencies are and how they affect your financial well-being, and try to deal with those that create problems. Perhaps the best you can hope for, without spending five years in therapy, is to turn what were unconscious reactions into conscious actions. That will go a long way toward helping you take charge of your financial life.

Money-Attitude Analysis

The following test was prepared for this book by Mel Prince, an associate professor of marketing at Fordham University and an expert on consumer behavior and money attitudes.

This test differs from other money-attitude tests in that it doesn't look to place you into one specific category. Prince believes individuals' attitudes toward money are a mosaic of eight varied and sometimes conflicting traits: impulse spending, frugality, risk aversion, nest-egg mentality, gambling, self-esteem, control over one's own money, and contempt for money. Your answers to the following questions, then, needn't be consistent. Instead, they should reveal the mosaic of your attitudes.

Analyzing the Results

Each set of three statements is designed to reveal your tendency toward one of the eight money traits Prince has isolated. The first set tests your tendency toward impulse spending. The second set tests your tendency toward frugality. The third set tests the degree of your risk aversion. The fourth set tests how strongly you have a "nest-egg" mentality. The fifth set tests for a tendency toward gambling. The sixth set tests how strongly your money and self-esteem are tied together. The seventh set tests for your tendency to take control over your own money. And the eighth and final set tests how much contempt you have for money.

Each subtotal indicates the strength of your tendency toward that particular trait. A subtotal of from 3 to 6 indicates a strong tendency toward the trait. A subtotal of from 7 to 11 indicates a moderate tendency toward the trait. And a subtotal of from 12 to 15 indicates a weak tendency toward the trait. For example: If you scored a 4 on the first set it would indicate you have a strong tendency toward impulsive spending; if you scored a 13 on the seventh set you have a weak tendency toward being in control of your own money.

Surviving the Squeeze

		Agree strongly	Agree somewhat	No opinion	Disagree somewhat	Disagree strongly
1.	I often buy items I don't really need because they're on sale.	1	2	3	4	5
	I often get carried away when I shop.	1	2	3	4	5
	I tend to make financial decisions based on how I feel at the moment.	1	2	3	4	5
	SUBTOTAL #1 _____					
2.	I feel guilty when I spend money, even when it's for necessities.	1	2	3	4	5
	I tend to be very critical of the way I've handled my money matters.	1	2	3	4	5
	It bothers me to have to buy something when it isn't on sale.	1	2	3	4	5
	SUBTOTAL #2 _____					
3.	Negotiating the right price of a new car is a frightening experience.	1	2	3	4	5
	I don't like investments where there's a chance of losing money.	1	2	3	4	5
	I don't feel like I'm in control of my financial security.	1	2	3	4	5
	SUBTOTAL #3 _____					
4.	I feel it's important to have a large savings fund for emergencies.	1	2	3	4	5
	I often think about the investments I should have made.	1	2	3	4	5
	My parents taught me the wisdom of saving for a rainy day.					
	SUBTOTAL #4 _____					

Money Myopia: The First Hurdle

		Agree strongly	Agree somewhat	No opinion	Disagree somewhat	Disagree strongly
5.	I like to gamble, but I often get carried away.	1	2	3	4	5
	If I had enough money, I would quit work and live a life of leisure.	1	2	3	4	5
	I often buy lottery tickets in the hope of striking it rich.	1	2	3	4	5
	SUBTOTAL #5 _____					
6.	I feel if I had enough money people would give me the respect I deserve.	1	2	3	4	5
	I tend to measure a person's success by how much money he appears to have.	1	2	3	4	5
	I judge how successful I am by how much money I make relative to others.	1	2	3	4	5
	SUBTOTAL #6 _____					
7.	I need to be actively involved in my money matters.	1	2	3	4	5
	I always know how much money I have in my wallet.	1	2	3	4	5
	I tend to be very assertive in my money dealings with others.	1	2	3	4	5
	SUBTOTAL #7 _____					
8.	Most rich people are vulgar and disgusting.	1	2	3	4	5
	I only want enough money to give me the freedom to do what I really want.	1	2	3	4	5
	I feel fate plays a large part in how wealthy a person becomes.	1	2	3	4	5
	SUBTOTAL #8 _____					

Here's a simple chart you can use in order to take an overall look at your mosaic of money attitudes. Simply check off the degree of your tendency toward each of the eight traits.

STRENGTH OF TENDENCY

Money Trait	Strong	Moderate	Weak
Impulse Spending			
Frugality			
Risk Aversion			
Nest-Egg Mentality			
Gambling			
Self-Esteem			
Control over Money			
Contempt for Money			

The only traits you need to be concerned with are those you have a strong tendency toward. A strong tendency toward any of these traits could be damaging to your overall financial health and could inhibit your ability to survive the squeeze. Let me go over the traits one by one, explain how each could potentially hurt you, and offer some tips I've used to help baby boomer clients mitigate the harm.

If You Spend Money Impulsively

A strong tendency toward impulsive spending can lead to both overspending and inefficient spending. If you don't think about how much you're spending and just hand over your credit card, it's easy to spend more than you should; maybe even more than you have. If you don't deliberate over what to buy, it's hard to be sure you're getting the most for your dollar. And as you'll see in the coming chapters, in order to survive the squeeze you'll need to spend your money sparingly and wisely.

This is one of the most common traits my baby boomer clients discover in their self-analysis. It is not due to some generational character flaw but because they're the first generation to grow up totally at ease with credit cards and automated teller machines. Take Carol Novak, for example.

Carol is a single, thirty-five-year-old associate professor of literature at a major university. While she was otherwise savvy, her spending habits were out of control. A voracious reader and a lover of fashion, Carol spent most of her free time browsing through bookshops and clothing stores. Whenever she found something that struck her fancy, she'd pull a credit card out of her wallet and buy it. If the shop didn't take credit cards, she'd simply head over to the nearest cash machine and withdraw enough to pay for whatever had caught her eye—plus a little extra. After ten years of such impulsive spending, she had accumulated a sizable, high-interest credit-card debt. She came to me looking for help in putting her financial house in order.

I told Carol she needed to make purchasing more of a cognitive and painful act. Rather than using automated teller machines and credit cards—which allow money to be obtained and spent quickly—I told her to cash checks and then pay cash for everything. I suggested that while she was standing on that long line at the bank she'd have an opportunity to think about how much cash she was pulling out and what she was going to spend it on. When she got up to the teller's window, wrote out the check, and recalculated the balance in her account, she'd have a chance to directly see the impact of what she was doing. Then, when she got to a bookstore or clothing store and saw something she wanted to buy, she'd be forced to note the cost, look inside her wallet to see if she had enough money to cover it, calculate how much she'd have left after making the purchase, and finally decide whether or not she really needed or wanted the item.

All this extra time to think helped Carol cut her impulse spending by 75 percent.

If You're Excessively Frugal

Although many of life's joys—attending a concert, going on a vacation, owning a work of art—don't offer material rewards, they add immeasurably to the quality of our lives. There's nothing wrong with occasionally spending money on something frivolous as long as it's something you can afford and you don't make a habit of it. While there are a great many sacrifices required in order to survive the squeeze, neither baby boomers nor anyone else should have to live "on bread alone." Excessive frugality can also inhibit your willingness to consider investment opportunities.

That was the case with Marc Bennett. A forty-two-year-old marketing executive, Marc came to me to at the suggestion of another client, a woman to whom he had just become engaged. She explained that they were having problems melding their financial lives. I had them both come in and after a few minutes it was clear to me that Marc had a real problem parting with his money. He never bought anything that wasn't totally practical, even though he had a very large income.

I suggested to Marc that he make at least one small, frivolous purchase each week. If he had a hard time spending money on himself, I told him to buy something for his fiancée, his mother, or a friend. Or to give some money to the homeless. The purchase needn't be anything dramatic: A flower or a cookie would do. What mattered, I explained, was that he should give it for no reason other than that he cared for the other person.

After six months of such giving, Marc had changed quite a bit. He learned to revel in the warm responses of those he gave things to for no reason. While he's no spendthrift, he no longer hoards his money, and today he's happily married.

If You're Overly Risk-Averse

A strong tendency toward risk aversion keeps individuals from taking full advantage of all their opportunities to grow wealth, which, as I'll explain in chapter 9, is a vital part of surviving the squeeze. If you're overly afraid of risk, you won't be able to grow wealth at all. Money that is totally safe—let's say, hidden under your mattress—shrinks in value due to inflation. Money that is almost totally safe—let's say, kept in a simple bank account—earns interest, but at best it only just keeps pace with inflation. It may not shrink in value, but it certainly doesn't grow. Only money that is risked, or in another word, invested, will outpace inflation and actually increase in value.

Sometimes just explaining this helps my clients who are overly risk-averse. But in the case of Barbara Levine it wasn't enough. Barbara is a forty-three-year-old executive assistant who was widowed in her late thirties. She was left with one son and a great deal of life insurance money and came to me at the suggestion of another financial adviser who was having difficulty convincing her she needed to be less conservative in her investing.

After double-checking that she indeed should take on more risk, I explained to her what I outlined above—that money must be risked in order to outpace inflation. When she remained reticent, I probed a bit deeper and found that she was afraid of trusting investment advisers' judgment of risk. I told her that she needn't look to an investment adviser for that analysis; she could do it herself. One of the fixed laws of capitalism, I explained, is that the higher the potential yield on an investment, the greater the risk involved. All she needed to do to determine the level of possible risk was to look at the possible reward. Once she accepted this, she no longer needed to fear false advertising: The more con men inflated claims of rewards, the more they'd actually be demonstrating the potential risks.

Now, two years later, Barbara is on the way toward growing a solid future for herself and her son through sound management of risk.

If You Have a Nest-Egg Mentality

Those who are obsessed with establishing and maintaining a nest egg of savings are combining risk aversion and excessive frugality. This is the worst possible combination of traits, for not only are they missing out on opportunities to grow their wealth, which they'll need to do in order to survive the squeeze, but they're also missing out on opportunities to use their money to get and give pleasure.

I've come across only a few boomer clients who have this tendency, but one who sticks out in mind was Lisa Stone. Lisa is a thirty-six-year-old graphic designer. The building in which she was renting an apartment was being converted to a condominium. Her neighbor felt it was an exceptional opportunity but couldn't get Lisa to listen to reason.

After verifying that it was indeed a good buy, I spoke to Lisa about her fears. I discovered she was the youngest of seven children of older parents who were adults during the Great Depression and World War II. She had been brought up with an excessive fear of financial disaster. I explained to Lisa the disadvantages of simply saving money and pointed out how she could take simple yet accurate readings on the risks of various estimates by looking at their potential return. Then I encouraged her to make at least one frivolous purchase each week, if not for herself, for her family.

While she was still hesitant, after two months she was able to overcome her fears and buy her apartment.

If You Tend Toward Gambling

A tendency toward gambling can be the most dangerous type of money myopia, leading to the ruin of both the individual and his family. Gambling is actually antithetical to my program for surviving the squeeze, since it amounts to letting your emotions rather than your logic take total control of your money decisions.

If the condition is truly compulsive, the only answer I can

offer clients is to enter a Gamblers Anonymous program and get help immediately. But if their tendency isn't that extreme, I can offer some guidance.

Michael Martin didn't bet on the ponies, but he had a tendency to take on excessive risk. A born entrepreneur, Michael, forty-five, was a very successful small-businessman. But rather than being prudent with the proceeds from his business, Michael threw his money into high-risk investments and get-rich-quick schemes. A mutual friend suggested he come to speak with me, ostensibly about his business. But after a few hours with him, I realized Michael's business was fine; it was his attitude toward money that was a problem.

I pointed out to Michael something he already knew but hadn't internalized: The extraordinary returns being offered by the investments he was pursuing automatically carried with them extraordinary risks. Then the two of us calculated exactly how much time it would take Michael to earn back all the money he had already lost. In effect, he would be working another five years just to recoup his losses. I suggested that if he continued to take such risks, he would eventually run out of time to recover from them, leaving himself and his family in a financial hole.

Realizing that he couldn't risk beyond his ability to rebound from losses, Michael began to change his investment life. Of course, he's still enamored by high-risk/high-reward investments, but he no longer puts the majority of his money into them.

If You Use Money to Boost Your Self-Esteem

Most of us occasionally use money to boost our self-esteem. However, if money becomes our sole or most important measure of self-worth, we're money myopic. Linking money this closely with self-image won't allow boomers to give up all those false assumptions they've acquired and will therefore prevent them from implementing a program to survive the squeeze.

Many of my boomer clients vacillate in the degree to which they have this tendency. At some point in their lives they've become obsessed with money as a status symbol, while at others they've rejected the idea that their worth as a human being is tied to their financial net worth. This mirrors a continuing shift in overall generational values between the asceticism of the 1960s and the conspicuous consumption of the 1980s. While most of my clients today seem to have reached some middle ground, I do still find some whose self-image is still tied closely to their money.

Stan and Carol Kaplan came to me for help in buying a second home. Stan is a forty-five-year-old stockbroker; Carol, a forty-two-year-old antiques dealer. They have no children. In the process of advising them, I realized that both their self-images were linked to their money. Rather than making financial decisions based on their needs and wants, they were factoring in issues of status. For instance, they wanted their second home to be in a "name" town regardless of whether or not it made sense financially. Once I realized what the problem was, I explained how it could cause them severe trouble down the road and offered some suggestions.

First, I told them to prepare two lists, one of famous people throughout history who had little or no money and another of equally famous figures who were wealthy. I then asked them to decide which list contained the most significant individuals. Even after a cursory examination of the lists, they saw that people like Henry Ford, J. Paul Getty, John D. Rockefeller, or even Andrew Carnegie weren't anywhere near as significant as Moses, Jesus, Buddha, Gandhi, Martin Luther King, Mother Teresa, or Henry David Thoreau. While it's an obvious exercise, the moral of it is important: A person's value has more to do with spiritual than financial wealth.

Next, I asked Stan and Carol to draw up another list, but this time of all the things they'd buy to boost their self-esteem or status. I told them to be sure to include all the specifics, like size, manufacturer, and location. After they finished their list, I told Stan and Carol to go back and come up with a bigger, better, or more expensive version of each item. I had them repeat the process twice and then pointed out that it could go on forever. I suggested that no matter what they possessed, there would always be something bigger, better, or more expensive. That's how capitalism operates. I told Stan and Carol that I believe that those who measure their self-worth through money can never really be satisfied.

"But, Stephen," Stan said, "I really must maintain the standards of the people in my peer group." I referred Stan back to the first exercise and asked him which of the two lists he'd rather be associated with: the one containing J. Paul Getty or the one with Buddha. He didn't answer. I took his silence to mean he'd rather hang out with Buddha and proceeded with the consultation. I knew that if he'd really rather pal around with Getty, his money myopia was too deeply ingrained for me to be able to help him.

If You Want to Exercise Excessive Control Over Your Money

This trait becomes a problem only if you are so concerned about maintaining control over your money that you can't let your mate pay the bills or you can't stand a mutual fund manager selecting the stocks or bonds in which your money will be invested.

That was the case with Nick Amato, a forty-three-year-old law enforcement officer. He and his wife, Fran, came to me for help in buying a home. The first sign of trouble was that Nick didn't think it was necessary for Fran to come along to the consultations—he relented only after I insisted. In our meetings I saw that Nick was a money-control freak. Not only wouldn't he give me the full details of his money; he had a hard time even letting his wife become involved.

I explained to Nick that just as he wouldn't operate on his own brain, he couldn't be entirely self-reliant when it came to money—at least not if he wanted to survive the squeeze. I pointed out that unless he became a professional money manager, he'd have less knowledge than those he could hire. I suggested to Nick that the most effective way for him to exercise

Couples and Money

I always insist that I meet with and advise both partners in a relationship. That's because partners have an interesting effect on each other's attitudes toward money. Couples have a natural tendency to polarize into opposites. An extreme attitude by one partner will force the other to take an equally extreme but opposite attitude in order to compensate and achieve a balance. When both partners have the same tendency, they often compete for sole possession of the attitude. The loser in such a battle—the partner who can't top the other's extreme behavior—will then take on the opposite attitude in response. For example: If a man with a slight tendency toward impulsive spending marries a woman with a strong tendency toward frugality, he may become more of an impulsive spender in order to balance her frugality. If two impulsive spenders get together, they'll go on a shopping spree until one gives up and begins pushing for frugality. In order for a couple to come to grips with, and compensate for, their money tendencies, both must go through the same process of self-analysis.

control over his own money was in the selection and supervision of his professionals.

While Nick still calls more often than the average client, in the past year he has learned to delegate some control over his money to his professional team.

If You Have Contempt for Money

Those who have contempt for money are making the same mistake as those who tie self-esteem to it: They haven't depersonalized money. These individuals, however, believe that money is somehow corrupting or evil. They identify strongly with all the individuals on the list of important people who had little or no money but mistakenly believe that the value of these marvelous individuals actually came about because of their poverty. Those who are contemptuous of money will never be willing to dedicate the time and effort required to take control of a tool that can, when properly used, help better their lives.

That was certainly the case with Dave Connors and Tom Campbell, two clients of mine. Dave and Tom continued to identify strongly with the 1960s values of their youth. They were repulsed by the excesses of the 1980s and saw the shift away from conspicuous consumption as somehow being a reaffirmation of their own beliefs. They treated their financial resources (which weren't meager) with disdain. They came to me for help in buying a farmhouse in the country. After just a cursory examination of their finances, I could see how inefficiently they were using their money as a tool to improve their lives.

I suggested that Dave and Tom engage in a bit of creative daydreaming. I told them to pretend that they had just inherited $100 million and then to come up with a list of things they would do with the money. Dave and Tom thought of wonderful uses for this newly found money, such as giving it to AIDS researchers and the homeless. I then suggested that their ideas were proof that money could be used for good purposes. I pointed to the success of Ben and Jerry of Ben & Jerry's Homemade Inc. and Patagonia, the outdoor-clothing company, proof that making money and doing good are not mutually exclusive. Finally, I asked Dave and Tom if they could name any greater good than using every tool available to do all they could to care for their loved ones.

While they'll probably never become captains of industry, Dave and Tom have begun to actively use their money as a tool, investing in what they consider to be socially progressive mutual funds and using it to better the lives of themselves, their families, and their friends.

None of the exercises outlined in these examples are "cures" for money myopia. In fact, I'm not sure if money myopia can actually be cured. I'll leave that debate to the psychologists. What I *am* sure of is that an awareness of your attitudes toward money can help mitigate their negative impact on your financial decisions. Once you're aware of your potentially harmful tendencies, you'll be better able to free yourself from false assumptions, view your situation rationally, take charge of your money, and survive the squeeze. With your money attitudes under control, the next step in that process is to focus on the health of your most important financial resource, your stream of income.

Chapter Three

....

Securing Employee Income

Security today is what's between your ears.
—Dale Klamfoth, senior vice president of the outplacement
firm Drake Beam Morin

The second step in surviving the squeeze is to secure your stream of income. The single most important element in personal finance is stream of income: the flow of dollars from an employer, a business, or an investment portfolio into an individual's pocket. It is stream of income that pays for luxuries and necessities and provides funds to invest in order to grow wealth. That's why making sure it's secure is so important.

In this chapter I'll focus on how to secure employee wages: the source of most baby boomers' streams of income. In the next chapter, I'll explain how entrepreneurs can secure their streams of income. Whatever the source of *your* stream of income, I encourage you to read both these chapters. The line between entrepreneur and employee is blurring. Most employees today will become involved in at least one entrepreneurial effort during their lifetimes, and conversely, most entrepreneurs will become employees at least one more time in their lifetimes. Even if these shifts are temporary, knowing how to secure both types of streams of income is vital.

If you're like most of my clients, you grew up thinking that implicit in employment was a quid pro quo: As long as you did your job, your employer would take care of you. If you were a

....

blue-collar worker, you might get laid off when business slowed down, but invariably you'd be rehired when business picked up. If you were a white-collar worker, you might not always get big pay raises, but you'd always receive at least a cost-of-living adjustment. Whatever the color of your collar, you thought the only reason you'd be "terminated" would be for doing something wrong.

These illusions were painfully shattered in the late 1980s and early 1990s when either you, or people you knew, were terminated without cause and without any hope of being rehired. Employers, both large and small, decided that the only way they could survive the economic downturn of that time and flourish in the future was to permanently downsize and tear up the implied contract that existed between employer and employee. That has left most baby boomers in a state of panic. Without a secure stream of income the pressures of the big squeeze are magnified.

Securing employee wages requires a two-step effort. In the short term you must make sure that your current job is as safe as you can possibly make it. And if you can't make it safe, you must do everything possible to minimize the pain of termination. These efforts will give you the time to focus on the second step: a long-term effort to adapt to the new American employment environment and use it to your advantage.

The Short Term: Making Sure Your Current Job Is Safe

Just as you abandoned false assumptions about your financial responsibilities for your parents, your children, and your own retirement, so, too, must you discard mistaken assumptions about your stream of income. No matter what type of organization you work for, no matter what title or position you may have, no matter how good you are at what you do, and no matter how long you've been there, you do not have job security.

While no two experts agree on what to call this new

arrangement, there's a consensus about what it entails. Today your employment with any one company depends on the complexity and importance of the particular project you're working on. In effect, you're like a free agent in professional sports. You, and everyone else in the company, must constantly prove your value each and every day.

That's very difficult for those who have been on the job for any length of time. It's human nature to become complacent in situations that become routine. Unless a conscious effort is made to stay fresh, we all fall into a comfort zone after a year or so. It is those who are in the comfort zone that are the prime candidates for layoffs. In effect, they've stopped trying to prove their value. If there's a decline in the company's fortunes or a change in management personnel or philosophy, they'll be the first ones to go.

Make a Fresh Start at Appearance and Behavior

The first secret to maintaining your current position is to mimic the behavior of individuals who are forced to prove their value: the newly hired. Get out of the comfort zone and recapture the spark you had on your first day on the job. Act as if every day were your first on the job.

❖ *Dress your best every day.* Remember how long and hard you thought about and worked on your appearance when you applied for this job and when you showed up for work the first day? Starting tomorrow, you should do the same. Nothing about your appearance should mark you as being complacent.

❖ *Maintain your appearance throughout the day.* When you were first hired, you didn't stop worrying about your appearance once you made it through the door in the morning. Make it your business to brush your teeth after lunch and to do your hair or shave again if necessary. If the company uniform is a suit, it's okay to take your jacket off when you're at your own desk, but as soon as you leave your work space, put it back on.

Refrain from rolling up sleeves, loosening ties, or kicking off shoes. If your clothes aren't comfortable enough to wear all day long, get new ones.

❖ *Act upbeat and enthusiastic.* When you first started, you instinctively knew that your outward actions were important to how you'd be perceived. They still are. Slap a happy grin on your face. Those in the comfort zone have, at best, vacant stares or, at worst, frowns on their faces. Most supervisors have the mentality of first-grade teachers: They think a smiling face means a happy person and a happy person means a productive employee. They'll see you smiling and think you're automatically adding to the bottom line.

❖ *Go by your supervisor's time clock.* Make sure you're in early every morning and leave late every afternoon. You don't need to be the first in or the last out. You simply need to shift your focus from the clock on the wall to your supervisor's work clock. Arrive before she does so that she'll see you at your desk when she comes in and leave after she does so that she'll see you still at your desk when she leaves.

❖ *Act like a team player.* Never complain about assigned tasks, no matter how boring, time-consuming, absurd, or unnecessary they are. Don't take an active part in office-gossip sessions. Listen and absorb any valuable information that's floating around the coffeepot or copying machine, but don't voice opinions yourself. Certainly don't take part in any backdoor maneuvers or back-office mutinies.

❖ *Ignore any negative comments about the changes.* Such changes in your appearance and behavior may spark curious or condescending comments from peers, especially those who are still in the comfort zone. Shrug off the remarks. Keep up the new look and behavior for a week and the comments will cease. By that time you'll be well on the way toward convincing your superior that you're a model employee.

Make a Fresh Start at Performance

The second secret to securing your current job is to back up your changes in appearance and behavior with some real, substantive changes. These will underscore your supervisor's perceptions that you've changed. Substantive changes will cast your new job persona in granite. Once your supervisor has something concrete with which to back up her perceptions, you'll be as safe as you possibly can be.

❖ *Become a student of your company and industry.* Learn more about what is going on than what you hear in the office. Subscribe to and read the leading trade magazine. Read books about your industry. Find out what others, especially the analysts, think about your industry and company. Attend trade-association meetings. Read the company newsletter. Don't worry about broadcasting your newfound knowledge; it will come out naturally.

❖ *Look to broaden your responsibilities.* When you see a vacuum in the company, ask to fill it. As long as you don't take responsibilities away from others forcefully or immediately ask for added compensation for your new responsibilities, your taking charge will be seen as entirely positive.

❖ *Add to your bundle of job skills.* Take advantage of any company education and training programs that exist. If there are none, study on your own. There are two routes to take here: Either pursue ancillary skills, such as writing, speaking, technology, or a foreign language, or learn about an area of business you're not that familiar with. For example, if you're in finance, study marketing or management. Perhaps the best way to decide what course of study to follow is to ask your supervisor or someone in human resources for advice on what would make you more valuable to the company. That will clearly let them know you're seeking to make yourself a more valuable employee.

❖ *Establish or fortify your power base.* If you have customers or clients who are personally loyal to you, ask them to write "unsolicited" letters on your behalf to your supervisor. If you don't have a natural power base, create one, perhaps drawing on one of your new responsibilities or added skills. See if your peers can be transformed into a power base perhaps by helping them in substantive ways.

❖ *Offer suggestions to improve the bottom line.* Suggest ways to save money, make more money, or best of all, save time. Time-saving suggestions have the greatest impact, since they have a double effect: Not only do they save money; they also provide the chance to make more of it.

Meet with Your Supervisor

After implementing both perceptual and substantive changes, it's time for the final step: a one-on-one meeting with your supervisor. The only way to make sure your changes in appearance, attitude, behavior, and performance have been noticed is to directly bring them to your supervisor's attention.

Schedule the meeting at your supervisor's convenience. Remember: The best time for such heart-to-heart conversations is probably before the workday actually begins, and the best days are Tuesday, Wednesday, and Thursday. (Of course, take your supervisor's individual idiosyncrasies into account.)

Take the direct approach. Explain that you love your job and that your supervisor's opinion is very important to you. Say you just want to make sure you're doing everything you can to contribute to the company's success. If necessary, detail all the things you've done. Basically, you're inviting your supervisor to give you an unscheduled, positive job review. If nothing else, it will force your supervisor to focus on your value to the company and will ensure that you're as safe as possible.

The worst thing that could come from such a meeting is that your supervisor may point out some areas in which she thinks you've been deficient. And that's not such a bad thing to have happen. It could serve as a very early warning of an impending layoff, allowing you to prepare. It also provides you with the opportunity to directly address any real or perceived deficiencies and then return to your supervisor for confirmation that you've overcome these shortcomings.

One further word of advice about this meeting: If you suspect your supervisor is in jeopardy, don't simply bypass her. Instead, use your conversation with her as a warm-up and then repeat the process with a personnel executive. If you need an excuse for speaking to personnel, say you need to ask about what types of continuing-education courses you should pursue. Once you're sitting down with someone in personnel, you can easily segue into the rest of your presentation.

This short-term securing of your current stream of income can be a bit humbling and at times may seem somewhat hypocritical; nevertheless, it's worth the effort. Without a secure stream of income you'll need to worry about how you and your family will pay for food, clothing, and shelter. Unemployment is the ultimate big squeeze. Even that, however, isn't insurmountable.

The Short Term: Making the Best of Termination

For some it might be too late to secure a current position. Perhaps the decision was made prior to your coming out of the comfort zone. Maybe an entire department is being cut regardless of how much individuals contribute to the company. Or it could be that a decision was made by someone so far removed from the situation that no amount of individual effort would make a difference. Whatever the case, it's important to realize that termination is neither a black mark against you nor a death sentence. It can be overcome just like any other obstacle in your path.

The first secret to effectively dealing with termination is to realize that in the 1990s there's some truth behind every rumor. That makes it imperative to learn how to spot the early warning signs of layoffs.

Read the Warning Signs

The first signs usually begin about four months prior to any staff changes. The signals will be subtle at first, directed at entire departments or divisions. This is the stage at which decisions are being made about which departments within the organization will be cut. Travel plans will be scaled back, and those still traveling will be told to fly coach rather than business class. Staff will be told to use overnight mail rather than messengers and second-day rather than next-day delivery. A memo will circulate encouraging use of the mail rather than the fax machine. Another will follow reminding staffers that company telephones are for business, not personal, use.

Next, rumors will begin to circulate around the office that business is down and some support staff will have to be cut. It will become harder to get approval for hiring temporary workers. Words like restructuring will pop up in conversations. Doors that once were always open will now be shut. Few people from other departments will drop by; and those who do will be curt. The only visitors who linger will be supervisory personnel, probably from the finance department. In fact, they'll be very talkative and show more interest in what you and your peers are doing than they ever did before.

The next set of warning signs involves a shift from the general to the personal. This is the stage when decisions are made about who within the department will get the ax. Supervisors' attitudes will seem to change overnight. People will avoid eye contact and will not smile when they pass in the hall. No one will stop by to make small talk. You will find yourself left out of meetings. Others will begin to get credit for your work. People will stop speaking when you enter a room. A project you're working on will be canceled but not replaced with another. Some of your responsibilities will be taken away and given to others. Supervisors will begin to point out specific mistakes that you've made. Your memos will go unanswered, and you will have a hard time getting an appointment to speak to any superior.

The third and final set of warning signs is anything but subtle. At this stage the decision as to who will be let go will be made. The company will now lay the groundwork for dismissal and prepare for what comes after. You'll be told to postpone hiring an assistant until after the holidays. You'll be asked to prepare a list of the projects you're working on, noting how long it will take you to complete each. Your periodic review will be canceled or postponed, or you'll receive your first negative review.

React to the Warning Signs

As soon as you pick up any warning signs on the job, no matter how subtle, it's essential you begin preparing. Denial is very common in these situations, so I believe it's better to be oversensitive and overreact than to take it easy and assume the rumors aren't true and the warning signs are all your imagination. Here are the steps you should take:

- Take home your Rolodex or address book and photocopy it.
- Compile a list of people whom you would call if you lost your job.
- Call those people now so that your contact with them later won't be a bolt out of the blue, and keep up regular communication.
- Take home a copy of your employee handbook and read the sections on termination and severance. If you don't have your own copy, go to the human resources department and ask to see one.
- Take notes on the relevant sections, date them, and make a note of your actions on your personal appointment calendar. You're dating your information just in case the company decides to change the rules without letting anyone know.

- If you have sick, personal, and vacation days coming to you that don't accumulate, take them now. Just make sure you're not too obvious about it—that means no Fridays and Mondays. If they do accumulate, don't take them unless you absolutely must.
- Take out your old résumé. Don't worry about rewriting it; simply bring it up-to-date.

Next, analyze your personal finances. You should have enough liquid assets to pay from six to nine months' worth of your personal expenses. Don't count on unemployment benefits as anything more than a stipend. If you don't have enough money available, start building your reserves. Here are some suggestions (you'll find more in chapter 5):

- Cut back on your personal expenses.
- Trim your insurance coverage and boost your deductibles.
- Find out about the rules on raiding retirement savings, pension plans, and investment accounts.
- Pay off high-interest credit-card balances.
- Think about establishing personal and home-equity credit lines now, while you're still employed and your chances of obtaining credit are still good.
- If you're female, gay, disabled, foreign-born, or over fifty; if you have worked for the same company for five years or more; or if you're a member of a religious, ethnic, or racial minority, contact an attorney who specializes in labor law. Whether or not you believe your termination may be discriminatory, your status provides you with added leverage that an experienced attorney can help you use to your advantage.

Launch a Preemptive Strike

Once you've accomplished all this, I suggest you give serious thought to launching a preemptive strike—directly approaching management with your fears before they have a chance to approach you—even if the signs are very subtle. There are some definite advantages to beating the other side to the punch. First, if the warning signs were intended for someone else, it could cut short your fears without any risk: the worst thing you could be accused of is oversensitivity. Second, if your suspicions are confirmed, you'll be throwing a monkey wrench into their plans, allowing you to take charge of the process and negotiate a severance package. And third, if your layoff was going to be part of a larger round of staff reductions, you'll now be able to negotiate your own deal rather than being forced to accept the same package as everyone else.

Of course, the preemptive strike will only work to your advantage if you're told the truth. You can count on human resources and personnel executives telling the truth, since they know that doing otherwise could lead to a lawsuit for unfair employment practices. But if there are no such people in your organization, you'll be forced to go to your immediate supervisor. In that case, you'll have to decide if your immediate supervisor is the type who will be honest or who will cover up until the end.

Ask for a Reconsideration

If you find out that you are, indeed, about to be terminated, you can ask for a reconsideration, even if it means taking a reduction in salary. By throwing yourself on the mercy of your supervisor or a personnel executive, you may be able to get yourself a probationary period. While on probation, you can do everything possible both to reverse the company's judgment and to look for another job.

Let me tell you about one client of mine who used this technique to great advantage. A well-respected book editor at a major publishing company, he learned through the grapevine one Wednesday afternoon that his superior was actively looking for someone to replace him. He came to me the next evening and asked what he should do. I helped him work out a script for a preemptive strike. On Monday morning he went in to meet his superior. He began by saying how much he loved his job and how he was disappointed in his own performance for the past couple of months. Without giving his superior a chance to interject, he went on to outline three new projects he had recently developed in an effort to boost the company's revenues. His superior was honest enough to say that she had been thinking of replacing him but now had decided to give him a month's probation. While my client rightfully looked on this as an insult, he smiled, thanked his boss for the second chance, and went right to work on four projects: the three he outlined to his boss and one of his own—looking for another job. At the end of thirty days his superior called him in to say she was lifting the probation. Ten days later my client went in to tell her that he had found another job and was leaving.

Negotiate Your Severance

One tactic you should certainly use, regardless of how you find out that you're going to be terminated, is to negotiate an increase in your severance. Severance pay is negotiable. You're actually in an excellent negotiating position, since there's nothing further your ex-employer can do to you. If possible, postpone discussing severance until you've had a chance to think about and formulate your requests. Above all, refuse to sign any waivers or release agreements, whatever the threats, until you've had a chance to press your case.

Prior to your severance discussion draft a formal memo outlining what you'd like to receive. Make sure to provide sound reasons for every request and to include items that don't require an immediate cash outlay, such as continuation of health insurance coverage, use of office equipment and facilities, and career counseling. These may be easier to get than added cash. Use all the leverage at your disposal, including guilt. Press your case strongly but try to settle the issues at this meeting. It's important for you to put this job behind you and get on with your future.

The Long Term: Adapting to Free Agency

Whether you're successful in securing your current stream of income or not, you will eventually find yourself in the market for a new job. Remember: There is no more job security. Rather than working your way up a predetermined ladder of increasingly important and better-paying positions, your career today will consist of a series of moves from project to project, employer to employer, and perhaps even industry to industry. The odds are that you will work for at least five different organizations in your lifetime.

While this lack of security and stability is initially frightening, I think it's actually much better for all involved. Obviously, employers will have a great deal more flexibility. But employees will as well. Rather than relying on an employer, you'll be relying on yourself. That offers you greater freedom and greater control over your own destiny. In addition, this new system will, to a large part, reduce job discrimination. Employees will be judged solely on their ability to manage a project successfully, not on where they went to school, what they look like, or how old they are.

Just as a free-agent athlete signs with a team for a predetermined length of time and with a particular goal in mind, so you'll join a company to take on a specific project. When the athlete's contract runs out, he's free to sign with another team or rejoin his current team. His value in the free-agent market is determined by how well he performed the previous season. The same will be true of you. Once you've completed the project you were hired to work on, you can either be re-signed by the same company to work on another project or sign with a different company entirely. Your value will be determined by how well you performed on your most recent project. In order to make this new situation as advantageous to you as free agency has been to professional athletes and to secure your stream of income in the long term, you'll need to adopt a new set of attitudes and behaviors.

Develop a New Professional Persona

The first hurdle you'll need to overcome is your professional persona. Most employees identify themselves very closely with their employer. When you introduce yourself, I'll bet you say something like this: "Hi, I'm Jane Smith. I work at Microsoft as a marketing manager."

As a free agent, you'll need to focus more on yourself and less on your current employer. It's a subtle difference but an important one. In the age of free agency, when every job is a temporary project, closely identifying yourself with a particular position will be unhealthy and unproductive. The closer you tie your professional persona to a job, the more you'll feel its loss, and the closer you tie yourself to any one organization, the more your abilities will be measured by its health.

Instead of seeing yourself as an employee of a particular company, look at yourself as a professional with a unique package of skills. When introduced to someone, say, "Hi, I'm Jane Smith. I'm a specialist in the marketing of high-tech products, currently working for Microsoft."

Analyze Your Package of Skills

In order to apply this new self-image to your long-term career planning, you'll need to analyze exactly what your package of skills comprises. While there are hundreds of skills tests around, I think you can do this job just as well yourself.

Draft as comprehensive a list of your personal and professional achievements as you possibly can. It's important to include your personal achievements, since you may have skills that you haven't been able to use in your professional life. Write a sentence or two about each achievement, spelling out exactly what you did.

Then go through everything you've written and underline all the verbs you used to describe your actions. For instance, you may have "organized," "helped," "influenced," "created," "analyzed," or "produced." Those verbs are, in fact, your skills. And the achievements you've listed are the documentation of your skills. Save all this paperwork. It will serve as the basis of your new free-agent résumé.

Here's an example of a list of personal and professional achievements with the important verbs underlined. The subject, Seth Adams, was a salesperson for IBM until being laid off. Prior to that he worked for General Electric.

Professional and Personal Achievements of Seth Adams

1. While at **IBM,** I *persuaded* the sales department manager to adopt mobile sales procedures. Having succeeded at that, I *created* a mobile sales protocol, *developed* all the necessary forms, and *trained* my fellow salespeople in the system.

2. While at General Electric I *organized* sales-report data, *analyzed* how the information correlated with goals, and then *reported* my findings to the regional sales manager.

3. After college, I joined a literacy program and *taught* adults to read.

4. During college I *organized* and *led* Kappa Alpha Gamma fraternity's record-setting fund drive.

Analysis: My skills include analyzing and organizing information; developing or creating a response to whatever I find; reporting on my findings and convincing others of their merit; and then training individuals to implement the plan.

Look to Expand Your Skills

In the age of free agency the most successful people will be those with the largest repertoire of valuable skills. That's because the organization of the future, according to most of the experts, will be diamond- rather than pyramid-shaped. There will be very few executives on top and very few staff people below. Most of the employees will be mid-level people simultaneously responsible for making their own decisions and implementing them, generally through the use of high technology. That means the successful free-agent marketing expert will be someone able to generate and analyze data base information about customers, decide on the best way to approach them, and then produce the vehicle, let's say a newsletter, to make that approach.

Since multiple skills will be considered valuable, successful free agents will work at constantly expanding their skills through on-the-job programs, continuing education, and volunteerism. If you don't know how to create and analyze a spreadsheet, take the company-sponsored seminar on the new financial software. If you don't speak a foreign language, take a class in Japanese at the local community college. And if you've never had a chance to develop organizing skills on the job, volunteer to head up the fall fund-raising campaign for your favorite charity.

Similarly, in the age of free agency, horizontal reassignments may in fact be more valuable in the long term than new titles or slight increases in power. Walk through the company's offices and keep your eye out for niches that aren't being filled and openings in areas where you lack experience.

Make Sure You Have Benchmarks to Measure Success

Since advancement and compensation are no longer going to be based on attendance and endurance, you'll need to sit down with your supervisor and establish benchmarks for measuring your success. This conversation can take place either when you're securing your stream of income, when you're having your annual review, or when you're being interviewed for a new job. Rather than an ambiguous job description listing responsibilities, you want a set of specific goals. Once you achieve these goals, you can use your success to segue into another project either inside or outside the company or to justify an increase in salary.

Develop a Mercantile Attitude

Another change you'll need to make in order to succeed as a free agent is to develop what I call a mercantile attitude. Many of my baby boomer clients have consciously sought "meaningful" employment. Money was never a sufficient reason for them to do something. There was always an additional factor that entered into the equation. That other factor could have been that the job in question was prestigious or that it helped society in some way. Whatever the case, these individuals looked upon their job or business as being more than just the source of their stream of income. That's a wonderful attitude to have if you don't need to worry about your stream of income. I'll encourage all boomers to adopt this attitude when I address the issue (or nonissue) of retirement in chapter 9. But in order to become a successful free agent and survive the squeeze, you'll need to put that attitude on hold.

In your current situation you don't have the luxury of viewing your job as anything other than a stream of income. Titles are nice. Corner offices are enjoyable. Travel broadens the mind. Status does wonders for the ego. But let's face it: Only money puts food on your table. My advice is to make it clear to yourself and to others that you are doing your job for one primary purpose: to make money. That your goal is to make money doesn't mean you're a greedy, heartless, evil individual. I'm not suggesting you give up those other goals and desires. I'm simply saying they should all be secondary to the primary focus of your occupation: generating a stream of income.

Asking for a Raise

The most obvious way to get a short-term increase in your stream of income is to ask for a raise. Here are some tips:

• Don't worry about "the system." In most cases it's a smoke screen, and even if it exists, rules can be broken for special circumstances.

• The only good reasons for a raise are that you've solved problems, taken on more responsibilities, increased revenues, cut costs, or saved time.

• Document your claim and estimate your worth in the open market.

• Pick your spots based on your supervisor's daily and weekly schedule. If you know she's always harried on Mondays and likes to leave early on Fridays, avoid them. If you know she's usually most relaxed after lunch, try to be her first afternoon appointment.

• Frame this as a shared problem and refer to the company, not your supervisor, as your employer.

• Maintain eye contact; refrain from nodding; don't be

How do you put this money orientation in place? Simple: You see dollar signs everywhere. Let me explain. Every time you are confronted with a choice or a decision on the job, make sure that you weigh it primarily in financial terms. For instance, let's say your supervisor comes to your office one day, tells you the downtown office is in trouble, and asks you to take charge of it. You, of course, are flattered that she thought you were just the person for the job. You think there will probably be a title change involved in the shift. And you remember there's a gorgeous office downtown with a view of the river. None of these factors—not the ego boost, the status of a new title, or the luxury of a new office—should be the prime factor in your agreeing. You should do it only if the move makes economic sense. It tentative or project guilt; and, above all else, don't be humble.

- If the response is that you haven't been at the company long enough, say you don't think your contribution can be fairly measured by the number of months you've been there.
- If the response is that you haven't waited long enough since your last raise, say you don't think your added responsibilities can be measured by how long it has been since your last increase.
- If the response is no, based on policy or the need for fairness, ask if that means you won't be rewarded no matter how successful you are.
- If the response is that the company can't afford to pay now, negotiate now for a raise that will take effect at a definite date in the future and that might be retroactive.
- If the response is that the company can't afford to pay that much, expand the discussion to include things other than money, such as added benefits or responsibilities.

could make economic sense in the long term if it's an opportunity to either acquire or demonstrate new skills that could help you land another position. In the short term it makes economic sense if you'll be paid more money. The rest of the factors are like icing on the cake—nice to have but not essential.

You'd be amazed at how quickly such an attitude will have an impact on your life. In business there's an incredible amount of time spent trying to figure out what motivates others. The idea is to find out what someone else really cares about and then show him how taking a particular action will help him obtain what he wants. This goes for getting an employee to do something, a client to hire you, or a customer to buy your product. By subtly broadcasting that the primary factor motivating your decisions is money, you provide superiors, co-workers, subordinates, clients, and customers with the key to getting you to do what they want.

Let's go back to your boss's request for you to take over the downtown office. Assuming she really wants you to take the job, she needs to find your primary motivation. If she's unsure, she will probably fish around using a variety of different incentives. She may say it's a shorter commute. She may talk about the lovely corner office overlooking the river. She may talk about what your title would be. But if she knows you have a money orientation, she'll make sure it offers a salary increase that makes the move worth your while.

Let me tell you how this worked for one client of mine. A commentator on a cable television network, he was asked by the network's head of programming to take on a new assignment. My client expressed gratitude but immediately asked how this new responsibility would affect his career. The programming chief didn't understand right away. My client became more specific. He asked how this would affect his contract. The programming chief snapped at him: "Is money all you think about?" My client responded, "No. My concern is doing the best job I can and being adequately compensated for it." The programming chief stormed away. Two months later, another new assignment opened up, and when the programming chief presented it to my client, he made clear that it would mean a salary increase. My client accepted.

Take a Parallel Approach to Job and Career

It's very important to realize that your future does not necessarily lie with your current employer. Success on a particular project will not guarantee there will be other projects for you to take on at that company. That's why a successful free agent will take a parallel approach to all her actions. You'll need to ask not only how something will affect your job but how it will affect your ability to get another job. You'll need to focus on the health of your industry, not just your company. And you'll need to study how things are changing in the overall economy, not just in your industry. In effect, you are always looking for your next job. This doesn't mean you should curtail your on-the-job efforts. That would only accelerate the need to find another position. Instead, it means dedicating some of your time to long-term career planning.

A large part of your strategy will be the expansion and maintenance of a multidisciplinary network. Since you'll no longer be limited to a predetermined ladder within a particular industry, your network will need to embrace individuals at varied levels in different industries. Make it a practice to save the business cards of everyone you come into contact with on the job and in your personal life. Become involved in local politics or join charitable, service, or fraternal organizations. This multidisciplinary network will be vital when it comes time to shift industries.

The Long Term: Looking for a Job as a Free Agent

Now that the unwritten social contract between employer and employee has been torn up and replaced with free agency, boomers need to acquire some new job-search skills. That's because they probably will need to be prepared to shift industries frequently in response to economic currents.

Instead of trying to remain in an industry with few current or future opportunities, you can transfer your skills and experience to an industry that is doing better or is just emerging. If you used to work as marketing director for a bank, there's no reason why you couldn't become the marketing director of a health-services agency. If you previously did publicity for a publishing company, there's no reason why you couldn't do public relations for a private school.

Similarly, you could switch sides of a transaction. If you've been selling advertising space for ten years, you're entirely qualified to become an advertising manager for a company that buys ad space. If you've been a buyer for a clothing store for twenty years, you can easily become a manufacturer's sales representative, selling clothing lines to other buyers. In such a job search you'll even be able to fully exploit your existing network.

Another advantage to changing industries is that you'll stand out from other applicants. If you understand that you may be forced to take a cut in salary or responsibilities and are still willing to make the change, you may well become the most experienced person applying for the job. And while you may not have experience in this particular industry, the gap can be overcome through savvy research, résumé writing, and networking. Another way of overcoming the "no relevant experience" barrier is to find emerging industries in which no one has any experience.

Shifting industries can also be an interim step, allowing you to test potential career shifts. It will be easier moving from one career to another once you're in an industry. For example: A publicist will have an easier time becoming a teacher if she is doing public relations for a private school than if she is still touting books for a publisher.

Such a dramatic career shift is definitely a viable alternative today and shouldn't be dismissed out of hand. Some people— experts say as many as 20 percent—were in the wrong career to begin with. Many never really did any career planning. They picked their career because friends chose it, because their family had a history in it, or because it was the path of least resistance. Perhaps they started off in the right career but they, or the business, subsequently changed. You *can* shift careers; you're the sum total of all of your experiences both on the job and off, and you're getting wiser and more savvy as you get older.

Shifting industries requires a great deal of research, determination, and perhaps further education. You'll need to have a firm grasp of how your skills and experiences match the needs of the new field you're entering. You'll need to be able to look at ads for which you don't meet the criteria and deal with interviewers who are narrow-minded while continuing to believe you're not unqualified. You'll need to be willing to return to school if in fact specific criteria must be met. And if you're going to be shifting careers, you'll need to be willing to give up some money, power, and most of all, status. Years as a successful stockbroker are meaningless to an academic, just as a ream of published articles and teaching awards are meaningless to a Wall Street professional.

Research Industry Jargon and Company Needs

Whether you're going to be pursuing a position in a different industry or changing career directions, you'll need to begin by doing some research. This should take two directions: first, to ferret out the issues, major players, and jargon of the industry; and second, to understand the specific needs and dynamics of the companies that make up the industry. Having a working knowledge of the industry may consist of little more than adopting new buzz words, phrases, and acronyms and applying them to your own experience. These can be acquired through reading leading industry journals and attending workshops at relevant trade shows and conventions.

Specific knowledge of companies can be gained from reading annual reports. These will provide the names of the key company officials, hints on the philosophy and culture of the organization, information on the company's place in the industry, and tips on its health and finances. Trade shows offer an opportunity to read individual companies' sales and promotional literature, study their offerings, and observe their style. Trade magazines and journals can give you an idea of how each company in an industry fits into the overall picture.

The information you gain will not only provide you with a map of the industry; it will give you ample ammunition for later networking and job interviews. Two of the most common questions asked in such meetings are "What do you know about our industry or company?" and "Why do you want to work in this industry or for this company?" If you can launch into an informed and somewhat detailed discussion of the industry's or company's needs, you'll have gone a long way toward overcoming the "no relevant experience" hurdle. That can make the difference between being pointed in the direction of job opportunities or brushed off or between being the winner or an also-ran in a job hunt.

Free-Agent Résumés

Even though free agents will be concentrating on networking rather than answering advertisements to get their next project/job, a résumé is still essential. Since it is often used to weed out unqualified candidates, it can get your foot in the door; since it is often used as the basis for an interview, it offers you some control over the process; and it serves as a memory jogger after an interview but before a final decision has been made.

What's clear is that one size no longer fits all. Free agents' résumés must be elastic documents, easily adaptable to various industries and companies, that are constantly being revised. Remember: From now on you're always looking for a job.

There really is no one set formula for a free-agent résumé. Whatever works, works. That said, there are some guidelines to keep in mind.

- Regardless of how vast your experience, your résumé shouldn't exceed two pages (unless long, detailed documents are traditional in the industry you're looking to enter—academia and medicine, for example).
- Even if you're looking for work in a creative field, your résumé should appear traditional—no pink paper, calligraphic type, or gimmicks. Stick with good white paper, black print, and a conservative typeface.
- Don't include specific mentions of your age, sex, height, physical limitations, weight, race, or religion. A particularly cautious employer may discard a résumé containing such information for fear it could lead to a discrimination charge.

- At the same time, don't try to obscure anything by deleting information. Obvious omissions are red flags for the person doing the screening. If they don't want to hire someone like you, they won't, whether or not they base their discrimination on a résumé or an interview. Besides, you don't want to work for a discriminatory company.
- Highlight your accomplishments and show a progression of skills, not a chronological advancement in job titles. Accomplishments should center on three areas: making more money, saving money, and saving time.
- Describe these accomplishments in somewhat vague language, stating what you accomplished but not how you did it. You want the person scanning the résumé to wonder how you were able to cut two weeks off a magazine's production cycle, hopefully leading them to call you in and ask.
- If you feel the need for some type of introductory paragraph, consider a profile rather than an objective. If your objective doesn't match the interviewer's, you've no chance at an interview. A brief one- to three-sentence description of who you are and what skills you possess should be sufficient.
- Few prospective employers actually read information on an applicant's interests, but those who do look for specific information. That's why if you're going to include a section outlining your personal interests, they should be described in specifics rather than generalities. Don't just write reading or painting. Instead, write nineteenth-century detective novels or German Expressionist painting. If nothing else, it shows that you are an interesting person, and who knows, if the person scanning the résumé shares your interest, it could lead to an interview.
- If you're going to include sports on your list of interests, give some thought to exactly what type of sporting interest you include. Playing team sports, such as basketball and softball, indicates you have the ability to work with others. Mind games, such as chess and bridge, demonstrate analytic skills. Endurance sports, such as bicycling and

running, show determination and indirectly tell the prospective employer you're in good health and don't smoke.

Rolodex Renting

Most boomers are experienced at networking. However, they have generally limited their networking to their own industry. That's why I suggested earlier that you develop a multidisciplinary network as soon as possible. If you haven't had a chance to do that yet, you can use a variation on networking called Rolodex renting. This involves contacting everyone you know well and asking them if they have any contacts in the industry you're interested in—in effect, you're borrowing their Rolodex.

Since you're crossing industry lines, don't limit this fishing expedition to just co-workers and business peers. Speak to old and new friends, your family, college classmates, neighbors, professional advisers, past and present mentors, members of your church or temple, as well as fellow volunteers at a charitable organization. Use a simple, honest approach in your requests for contacts. Some people have even been successful using their college alumni directory to generate leads. As you compile your list of names, keep track of who gave you the name—that's your ticket into a meeting.

Maintain the Illusion of Informational Interviews

Once you get an appointment for a meeting, remember that you have two goals: You're both gathering information and advice and looking for a job. It's important, however, to maintain the illusion that this is solely an informational interview. Take your questioning of these individuals seriously. If nothing else, it will expand your knowledge of the business, which can lead to a fine-tuning of your résumé and a better discussion with the next contact. The subtext of the meeting is clear but should never be spoken. That makes things more comfortable for both parties. If you don't ask for a job, you won't be rejected. And if the person you meet with isn't asked, she won't need to reject you.

Overcoming the "No Relevant Experience" Hurdle

After going through a few networking interviews, you should be fairly confident about your interpersonal skills by the time a job interview comes along. However, be prepared for your "lack of relevant experience" to become an issue. This is less of a hurdle than you may initially fear. Clearly, someone in the organization was able to see the connection your résumé made between your skills and their needs, since you are in fact being interviewed. At this point you need to demonstrate your understanding of their industry by mentioning what you consider are the major issues and problems they are confronting. Then show how in your past career you have addressed and overcome similar obstacles.

By making your current position as safe as can be, by minimizing the damages of termination if you can't, by adapting your attitudes and behaviors for the age of free agency, and finally, by learning the new rules of looking for a job, you'll have done everything possible to secure your stream of income. The next step in surviving the squeeze is to make sure the stream of income you've just secured is being used wisely.

Chapter Four

....

Securing Entrepreneurial Income

*You can't simply do what your father did, or what you've
always done, or what your competitors are doing, if you want
to succeed in business today and tomorrow.*
— Dan O'Brien, director of the emerging business division of
the accounting firm Coopers & Lybrand

As an entrepreneur, you may not have to worry about being
laid off, but your stream of income is probably no more secure
than that of your employee-peers.

The world of entrepreneurs has changed just as dramatically
as the world of employees. Nearly all the basic assumptions un-
derpinning past practices and policies are becoming outdated.
Your customer, whether a business or a consumer, is increasingly sophisticated and demanding. He is holding you to higher
standards than ever before. And he is being pursued by others
not just from around the corner but from around the globe.
Many of the concepts on which you've based your business decisions in the past have changed, requiring you to basically re-
learn the rules while you're in the middle of running a business.
That has put your all-important stream of income in jeopardy.

Just as employees need to follow short- and long-term programs to secure their stream of income, so do entrepreneurs.
Your short-term program consists of determining whether your

....

business is worth saving and then doing everything possible to save it. Your long-term program consists of adopting a new attitude toward entrepreneurship and then implementing the new rules that go along with it.

The Short Term: Is This Business Worth Saving?

While baby boomer entrepreneurs won't need to humble themselves as much as their employee-peers, they'll need to be a lot more introspective and insightful during their short-term program. In order to secure your entrepreneurial stream of income, you need to reexamine your current business from top to bottom with a brutally honest eye and wield a very sharp, unemotional knife. That's because, in the final analysis, entrepreneurial income is secured only by the relative health of a business.

The first step in your short-term program involves some soul-searching. The question you're searching your soul for the answer to is "Should I even try to keep my current business up and running?" During the Reagan years it was tough not to make it in business; there was wind enough for even the smallest sail. Times have changed, however. Only the strong will survive in the 1990s and beyond.

In addition, the relationship of an entrepreneur to his business has changed. They are no longer inseparable. Your relationship to this business may well be finite. That's a premise I'll be stressing when we get to your long-term program, but for now let me just say that there may come a time when you'll need and want to start something else.

I suggest that if your current business isn't well positioned for success, you might as well sell it or shut it down and spend your energies on starting a new, properly positioned business. That way you'll need to make fewer compromises. In effect, you'll be starting with a clean slate.

What you're looking to determine is whether or not your

business is still viable. In order to determine that you'll need to have your computer or accountant generate up-to-date financial statements—a profit-and-loss balance sheet, accounts-receivable aging, thorough inventory analysis, and a list of customers' percentage contribution to your business. With the help of your financial advisers, examine the statements carefully. You're looking for evidence that your customer base is increasing, that you're keeping up with the competition, and that the business has been, and will continue to be, profitable. Have you been lending the business money to keep it afloat? Are you overly dependent on one or two clients? Does the business have the potential to grow, or is it just treading water? Does it need a few minor adjustments or a complete overhaul?

Be brutally honest about both the current health and future prospects of your business. There's nothing wrong with either pulling the plug or trying to sell a business that seems to have run its course. You need to begin to focus on your business as a source of a stream of income, not as your child. If you and your accountant concur that the business is still viable, you can heave a sigh of relief—but then take a deep breath. In order to make sure the business, and therefore your stream of income, stays healthy in the short term, you're going to need to kick some bad habits that many entrepreneurs picked up in the 1980s.

Short Term: Overcoming Complacency

Just as employees naturally become complacent after working in the same job for a period of time, so do entrepreneurs after being in the same business for a while. In the early days you watched where every penny was going. There wasn't an ounce of fat in your organization. You went over every order and every bill with an eagle eye. You had to because you didn't have a penny extra.

But then, thankfully, the business began to take off. You weren't as strapped for cash. You didn't need to run to the bank as soon as each check came in. You stopped going over the bills line by line. You probably even stopped reading the checks you were signing. That is all about to come to an end. These are volatile times for businesses. For you to be able to rely on your business to produce a secure stream of income, you must get back in touch with every detail of the operation and trim the fat that's built up.

That requires immersing yourself in the minutiae of your business—just as you did when you drew up your original business plan—going over those areas where you are most likely to have let some cobwebs accumulate.

Maximize Your Return on Cash While Maintaining Liquidity

The best place to start your inspection tour is at the top of your balance sheet, with the first item listed in the asset column: cash. In the early days you worried about not having enough cash. But today you probably have too much. You need to balance your need for liquidity against the possible interest you could be earning on your money if it were invested in the business or in a less liquid instrument.

Perhaps the best way to accomplish this subtle balancing act is to enlist the help of a banker or an accountant experienced in cash management. He should be able to help you set up a system in which cash is swept from your account at the close of business, invested in short-term commercial paper, and then returned to your account when you reopen. Such a system maximizes your interest while maintaining the necessary liquidity. In addition, the banker could help you avoid having others try to take advantage of you by "playing the float"—earning interest on your money by keeping it in their accounts longer than necessary.

Speed Up Collection of Your Accounts Receivable

After you've finished cleaning up your cash line, turn to your accounts receivable. This is where complacency becomes readily apparent. If you haven't already, date your accounts receivable.

A complacent entrepreneur lets accounts receivable age, failing to realize that every day over one month that he is owed money represents a substantial loss of money. Generally, this happens when the entrepreneur is no longer as strapped for cash as in the early days. He concentrates on generating sales and forgets that there's another part to the process: collecting.

Just to make sure your credit policies aren't somehow contributing to slow payment, contact your trade association and recheck the industry averages. Meanwhile, begin trying to collect those dollars due you. While you don't want to antagonize customers, it's important to remember that you're not in the business of lending money. Anyone who owes you money for more than thirty days is using you as a banker without giving you any collateral.

You shouldn't feel any qualms about asking for moneys owed you. Be polite but insistent. It is, after all, your money. If you must, blame the need for payment on someone else. Explain to those slow-paying regular customers that your banker is hounding you to speed up collections.

In addition, take this opportunity to make your credit policies toward new customers a bit stricter. Spell out the details up front. Ask any new customer without obvious credentials for a deposit equal to your cost plus approximate overhead expense. If the new customer objects or says that isn't possible, ask them to provide you with a letter of credit from their bank—or for a third-party guarantee—backing up their agreement to pay your bill. Both techniques offer increased protection without having to ask for cash on delivery and potentially losing the business.

Before leaving your accounts receivable, give some thought to whether or not you're overly reliant on one or two big customers. Do you have any clients who represent 5 percent or more of your billings? If so, begin to think about ways you can reduce your reliance on them. Think about developing a hit list and launching a new marketing or promotional campaign in order to bring in more clients and broaden your customer base.

Physically Examine Everything in Your Inventory

If you have any inventory, that's the next stop in your inspection tour. How long has it been since you and/or your accountant actually physically checked the inventory? For many businesses, taking inventory becomes more of a paper-pushing process than an actual examination. Not anymore. One of the secrets of breaking out of complacency is to shift from a "just in case" to a "just in time" mind-set about inventory.

As soon as possible, you and your staff must physically examine everything you have in inventory. Divide merchandise into "salable" and "no longer salable" categories. If you have too much of any one item—or too much of one size or color—categorize the overage as no longer salable regardless of its condition. Now, try to convert those no-longer-salable items into cash. There are actually a variety of ways. You could try to return merchandise for a refund. Perhaps if it's no longer salable because of its condition, you could have the manufacturer recondition, refurbish, or repackage it. Consider bulk selling of no-longer-salable merchandise at deep discounts. For example: If you have two thousand extra rolls of $5 slide film about to expire, shrink-wrap them in bunches of twenty and price each bunch at $25. Remember that you're really making money, not taking a loss, since if it wasn't heavily discounted, you'd get zero for the film.

Minimize Prepaid Expenses and Ask for Deposits Back

Turn next to any prepaid expenses or security deposits you have sitting on your balance sheet. Once again, these may be signs of complacency. Approach your landlord and utility and ask for your deposits to be returned. Point out that you've proven yourself to be a reliable customer. If you can't pry the money away from them, at least make sure you're earning real interest on it. Unless you save money by paying your insurance premiums up-front, you're paying the wrong way. Ask your broker to get you either a discount for prepaying or a no-interest quarterly payment plan. If he can't do either, see if another broker, perhaps someone with greater influence, can.

Stop Reflexively Buying Furniture and Fixtures

Next, turn your attention to furniture and fixtures. Here's another area of the business where complacency may set in. You have the money to buy something, so you do. Stop reflexively buying when you need it. There's an old business adage that I think makes more sense than ever today: Buy things that appreciate in value but lease things that depreciate in value. It's crazy to buy things just to have the depreciation. That's like spending money just because it's deductible. From now on stop buying. Sell off whatever you have that's obsolete and lease replacements.

Take Advantage of Accounts Payable Discounts

Turn next to the liabilities column of your balance sheet. The first item on the list is accounts payable. I'll bet you pay the bills—or more likely your bookkeeper does now—either fifteen or thirty days after they come in because it makes life easier. That's another sign of complacency. Let me explain.

If a vendor offers a discount for early payment, taking advantage of it can be a tremendous cash savings in the long term. If, for instance, a vendor you use monthly offers the traditional terms of 2/10, net/30 (meaning a 2 percent discount if paid within ten days and the total amount due within thirty days), you could save 24 percent (2 percent x 12 months) over the course of the year by paying promptly. If you're getting a better yield than that on your money, let me know about it. Of course, if a vendor doesn't offer a discount, it makes sense to pay at whatever speed is most comfortable.

Renegotiate Bank Debts If Possible

After establishing new accounts payable policies, take a look at your bank debts. If you have a loan with payments that are getting painful, now is the time to renegotiate it and, if possible, lengthen the term.

While you're at it, reexamine your relationship with your bank. I know you're probably on a first-name basis with your banker by now, but banks are looking for business today. It could be that the institution down the street may be able to do more for you.

Trim Your Payroll (and Keep on Trimming It)

If you're like most businesses, your largest expense is probably payroll. That's because nothing grows quicker than a staff. In the beginning there was just an entrepreneur. But as soon as he realizes he can't do everything on his own, he hires an assistant or a group of them. As soon as the assistants decide which areas of their jobs they like and which they dislike, they begin pushing for assistants of their own to take over the chores they don't like. As the business grows, more and more levels of employees are added, each wanting assistants of their own. Therefore, payroll always seems to grow at a faster rate than is actually necessary.

I believe it is almost always possible to cut staff by at least one position—if the entrepreneur is willing to take on additional responsibilities. Let's say you're a professional with an administrative assistant and a clerk. Your administrative assistant does ten things, two of which you used to do. The clerk does those things the administrative assistant had to give up in order to take on the two tasks you gave up. If you're willing to assume two tasks from your administrative assistant, it will free him up to take back the two tasks passed on to the clerk, enabling you to eliminate the position. The process is basically the same, albeit more complex, in a large organization.

My suggestion is to mentally rehire everyone in the company. Would you hire all of them today if they walked in off the street? After you've gone through this mental process, draw up a list of those you wouldn't hire today. Immediately lay off the one person from the list who is either the biggest troublemaker or the least well rounded. Do the firing on a Monday, if possible, so he can qualify for unemployment benefits right away and begin to take charge of his situation. (Consider going through this mental rehiring every six months.)

Simultaneous with the layoff, put a freeze on future hiring. Put the burden of proof on anyone who advocates adding a position, even if a new project comes in. Whenever possible, opt for part-timers or temporary employees, thereby saving yourself at least 20 percent in benefits. And when it comes time to issue raises, base them on this year's financial performance and the current cost of living rather than just replicating what you did in past years.

Ask Your Landlord for Concessions

After you've recovered from trimming your payroll, cheer yourself up by paying a visit to your landlord. Commercial rents have been in a free-fall for the past two years. Your landlord is, or at least should be, grateful there is someone renting his space at all. It's time to use your leverage and ask for some concessions. While you can try to obtain a lower monthly rent, I think you're more likely to be able to get a lease extension for the same rent or an agreement to make improvements to the property.

Put Your Insurance Policies Out for Bids

Next, put out your property and casualty insurance policies for new bids rather than just rolling them over. You may be able to trim up to 20 percent simply by adding an element of competition into your insurance budget.

Try to match that savings with a comparable cut in your benefit insurance package cost. Once again, rather than sticking with that old package you came up with five years ago, offer a smorgasbord of optional coverages to your employees. That will allow them to pick and choose what best suits their needs and yours to cut costs. Explore higher deductibles, coinsurance plans, and managed-care programs, such as health maintenance organizations and preferred provider organizations.

At the same time, contact local charities—such as the American Heart Association—and arrange for free health testing for your employees. You'll also save money in the long run by offering bonuses to those who either quit smoking or lose weight.

Reevaluate Your Marketing Program

Take a long, hard look at your marketing program. This is another area where old decisions tend to become etched in stone. When you first started, you had a real need for aggressive marketing, since you were an unknown. Today, if you've carved out a niche for yourself, your marketing needs may have diminished. As an established business, you should be able to come up with a direct correlation between any money you spend on marketing and your income.

Consider shifting your emphasis to public relations and publicity, which can be both less expensive and more effective than regular advertising.

Examine Every Other Expense

Go through each remaining line on your expense list. Rather than looking at what you're currently spending, start from scratch and ask yourself what really needs to be spent. Nothing is too small to escape a thorough examination.

- You can trim your business gift list and reduce the amount you spend on each gift—it really is the thought that counts.

- Go through your memberships and subscriptions, keeping only those things you truly need and use.
- Have the local utility conduct an energy audit and offer advice on conservation.
- Take advantage of employee environmentalism by setting up a system to recycle office supplies.
- Have staff parties at lunchtime in the office or store rather than after hours in a restaurant.
- Stop reflexively sending documents by overnight delivery services or via facsimile machines and instead reserve those expensive options for the few times when speed is really required.

Whenever you feel like a miser, remember that every dollar you save secures your stream of income. To keep employee morale from dropping, try to enlist their cooperation and support by offering low- or no-cost rewards for successful cost-cutting suggestions. For instance, offer to take the department that saves the most money out for lunch or give them an afternoon off.

Long Term: Shifting from Parent to Pilot

Just as employees must realize that they and their jobs are no longer one and the same, so entrepreneurs must begin to separate themselves from their businesses. That's a tough thing for most entrepreneurs to do, since the overriding mental metaphor they have for their relationship with their business is parent to child.

A business springs from an entrepreneur's mind rather than his loins, but that's about the only difference. The entrepreneur creates the business from nothing—in effect, giving it life. He invests not only his time and money but his heart and soul in the nurturing of the business. When the business is sick or hurting, the entrepreneur does anything and everything to make it well. The entrepreneur takes pride in the successes of the business and considers any rejection of it personally. Just as there's a physical and emotional link between parent and child, so, too, is there the same link between entrepreneur and business. But just as it's essential for the well-being of both parent and child for the cord to be cut, so, too, must the entrepreneur give the business an existence of its own.

You see, your business isn't your child. While it does represent a great deal of your personality and creativity, it's most important as a source for your stream of income. I'm not suggesting you devote any less of your efforts or energies to the development and operation of your business. And I'm not minimizing the importance of doing something you enjoy—in fact, that's something I'll stress in chapter 9. I'm simply saying that you need to put the business in its proper place. Its primary purpose is to provide you with a stream of income; everything else is secondary.

As soon as a business gets in trouble, the first instinct of most entrepreneurs is to cut their own salary. I suggest that's the last thing you should do. There are a million other ways to trim expenses, some of which I've already discussed in the short-term program. Instinctively cutting your salary in effect defeats the whole purpose of being in business, which is to provide an income for you and your family.

I think a better metaphor for your relationship to your business is of a fighter pilot to his plane. An aircraft is a tool. It provides the pilot with the means of completing his mission. Undeniably, a pilot develops some affection for his plane. It's not uncommon for the pilot to give his plane a name and to assign human qualities to it. In conversations with others the pilot may even reflect back on all the times the plane pulled him through some difficult situation and express gratitude to it. Yet when the plane is beyond repair or outmoded, the pilot doesn't sacrifice his own safety in order to keep using it. He either sends it to the junkyard or hands it over to someone else for a less demanding task and takes command of a new plane. And soon enough he's developing affection for the new plane and naming it as well. I think you should treat your business the way a pilot treats his plane. Think of it as a tool. Certainly you can develop affection for it and become attached to it. But don't let that affection and attachment stand in the way of your goals or success.

You need to have a dispassionate attitude toward your business and focus on its ability to produce a stream of income for you into the future. If you see that current trends bode ill for your future success, then it's time to react. You can shift directions if it isn't too drastic a change and if you'll be able to maintain your current goodwill. Or you can look to start another business either after selling or closing your current business.

There's nothing wrong with cashing out or shutting down and starting over. There's no shame in it. Some businesses have only a certain life span. Others may need the subtle tinkering that an entrepreneur may not have the personality to provide. Still others may need to be modified to keep up with the times.

For the long-term health of your stream of income you need to look at your business as a pilot looks at his plane. If it's doing the job you need it to do, keep using it. If it's starting to slow down but can be modified, do it. If it's no longer capable of doing what you need to have done, either sell it or scrap it and get a new plane.

Long Term: The New Fundamentals

After making sure your business is still viable, ridding yourself of complacency, and depersonalizing your relationship to the business, your final step in securing your entrepreneurial income is to learn the new fundamentals of doing business today.

Times have changed. The old rules, the ones you learned in business school or in the school of hard knocks, may no longer be valid. Here, according to my research and observations, are the new fundamentals of business that every baby boomer entrepreneur needs to be aware of.

❖ *Plan for unexpected change.* The days of regressive analysis as an accurate gauge of the future are gone. From now on, your business will need to be prepared for changes that can't be anticipated. That means it needs a company culture of flexibility and fast response.

❖ *Focus on the process.* Even though entrepreneurs themselves are project-oriented, their businesses should be process-oriented. The successful businesses of the future will be those that generate profits by stressing efficient operations and low expenses. Remember: It's much easier to control costs than it is to control revenues.

❖ *Strive for uniqueness.* The successful businesses of the future will be those with a clearly defined role and mission. It won't be enough to be just another liquor store, pizza parlor, or ad agency. Your operation will need to have a separate, distinct identity. Your goal should be uniqueness, so that you have no real competitors.

❖ *Concentrate on the core.* In order to succeed in the twenty-first century, businesses will need to concentrate on their primary function. Any functions that aren't part of the central operation should be farmed out or eliminated.

❖ *Think and act globally.* There's been a lot of talk about our living in a global economy and that this is the decade in which business owners will actually need to start putting their money where their mouths have been. Those who pursue foreign markets—either alone or with partners—who are open to foreign suppliers, and who investigate foreign capital will prosper. And that goes for every business, no matter how large or small.

❖ *Maintain a contingency reserve.* Massive societal bills are coming due, and one way or another, business is going to be asked to pick up some of the costs, whether it's for expanding our health-care system or modernizing our educational system. That means businesses will need to have some form of contingency reserve set aside to address these new demands or risk being bankrupted by their new "obligations."

❖ *Develop relationships with customers.* In the future it won't be enough to know where your customers live and what they watch, listen to, or read. Successful businesses will know what their customers are thinking, what they want, what products they buy, what the chances are of their switching vendors or brands, and what type of relationship they want from the company.

❖ *Be fair and flexible with employees.* There will soon be a shortage of skilled workers, making it essential for businesses to hold on to good people. That means your company must move beyond paternalism and develop some type of caring partnership with its staff. Options such as flexible time, part-time employment, and job sharing will need to be available.

❖ *Establish and maintain solid business partnerships.* No one will be able to succeed on his own in the future. Businesses will need to have strong relationships with other businesses, whether through joint ventures, strategic partnerships, or synchronized planning.

I realize these are rather abstract general principles. I'm offering them not as a blueprint for you to model your business on but as a guide. If you can see your current business measuring up in most of these areas, it has an excellent chance of making it in the future and providing you with a secure stream of income. But if it is still a creature of the 1980s, or earlier, it's time to turn it around or start from scratch. Whatever you do, the next step in the program to survive the squeeze is to make sure you get the most from your now secured stream of income.

Chapter Five

....

Making Your Stream of Income More Efficient

All decent people live beyond their incomes nowadays, and those who aren't respectable live beyond other peoples'. A few gifted individuals manage to do both.

—Saki (Hector Hugh Munro)

The third step in surviving the squeeze is to maximize the efficiency of your stream of income by controlling your spending.

Considering its importance, most people spend very little time examining their spending. I think that's because people instinctively fear that any attention paid to spending means sacrifice, deprivation, and the dreaded *b* word: budgeting. As you'll see by the time you finish reading this chapter, such fears are unfounded. In fact, by not focusing on spending, baby boomers are missing out on an opportunity to take charge of their lives.

You actually have a great deal more control over your spending than you do over your stream of income. While you can work to secure your income in both the short and long term, there is always at least one other person involved in the process whose behavior you can try to influence but can't control. If you're an employee, you must deal with at least one supervisor,

....

probably more. If you're an entrepreneur, you must deal with your customers and vendors. When it comes to spending, however, there's no one in charge but you. You're the one who decides to spend your money—no one else is in charge. Sure, there are attempts, often very persuasive ones, to encourage and influence your spending. But in the final analysis the decision is yours alone.

(If you're one of a couple, your partner can and should have as much influence over spending as you. But rather than get into the dynamics of relationships and money—the subject for another book—I'm going to address individuals in this chapter and assume that after one partner finishes reading, she will pass the book on to the other one. As far as your kids' spending goes, I'll be getting into that hornet's nest in chapter 8.)

And that decision is a vital one. The way you make your spending decisions determines how you lead your financial life. Your spending style dictates where, when, how, and why your money is and isn't spent.

Based on my experiences with clients, I believe most boomers are prepared to face up to the shortcomings of their spending style. That's because they instinctively know they must if they want to survive the big squeeze. Boomers cannot go on spending more while their incomes remain, in real terms, stagnant. The problem is, most of my clients don't know what to do about it. However, I do.

Three Steps to Savvy Spending

Spending is a lot like eating. When you know that you're eating too much, your first instinct is to go on a diet. That may work for a little while, but soon you're back to your old eating patterns. In order to truly change your eating habits, you need to understand why you're overeating and address those factors. The same is true for changing your spending style. The obvious response to the realization that you're spending more than you should is to budget. But such an approach invariably leads to failure. You can't just go on a budget and expect to undo a lifetime's worth of spending habits. In order to alter your spending style, you first need to understand the reasons for it.

I believe there are three distinct factors underlying most baby boomers' spending problems. First, most boomers are completely unaware of how much money they're actually spending and where it's going. Contributing to this lack of awareness is the second problem: Spending has been made pleasant and is looked upon as a social activity. And topping it all off is the third problem: Most boomers simply never learned how to be savvy spenders.

Time after time in my consultations with baby boomer clients I've come across these same difficulties. It didn't matter if the client was a middle-class computer salesman or a wealthy film actor. Nearly every one has had the same three core problems. I believe that's because many grew up in families that were moving up the economic ladder and in which the child's needs were often paramount. As a result, many boomers never needed to be aware of their spending. The increasing availability of credit and society's association of spending with the satisfaction of wants, not just needs, made spending fun rather than a task for most boomers. Finally, their parents' sudden affluence and understandable desire to shield boomers from deprivation led the silent generation to keep from passing on the savvy spending lessons they learned from their own parents. In order to change your spending style I suggest you take the pledge and jump into the following three-step program.

Step #1: Where Has All the Money Gone?

I'll bet you can't tell me where any more than 80 percent of your monthly income is going. I'm so sure I'll win the bet that I'll even help you come up with the numbers (see table 1).

TABLE 1. MONTHLY EXPENSES WORKSHEET
Monthly Take-Home Income

Daily Living Expenses

Food   _____

Clothing   _____

Child care   _____

Education   _____

Cleaning   _____

Cosmetics and toiletries   _____

Shelter Expenses

Mortgage/rent payment   _____

Homeowner's insurance   _____

Utilities   _____

Telephone   _____

Home furnishings   _____

Home improvement and repairs   _____

Medical Expenses

Doctors' and hospital fees   _____

Nonprescription drugs   _____

Health insurance   _____

Prescriptions   _____

Transportation Expenses

Auto fuel   _____

Auto insurance   _____

Auto payments   _____

Auto repairs   _____

Parking   _____

Toll   _____

Taxi fares   _____

Train and bus fares   _____

Entertainment Expenses

Books and recordings _____

Cable television _____

Dining out _____

Dues and memberships _____

Movies, videos, plays, concerts _____

Subscriptions _____

Take-out meals _____

Vacations _____

Other Luxuries

Charitable contributions _____

Jewelry _____

Gifts _____

Business of Living Expenses

Disability insurance _____

Life insurance _____

Property taxes _____

Professional services _____

Postage _____

Debt-Related Expenses

Banking fees _____

Credit-card interest _____

Daily Living Expenses _____

Student-loan payment _____

Other loan payments _____

Savings _____

Total monthly expenses accounted for _____

Discrepancy (monthly income minus
   monthly expenses accounted for) _____

Percentage unaccounted for _____
(discrepancy divided by monthly income)

I can almost guarantee you're unable to account for at least 20 percent of your income. Don't feel bad. I make the same wager with every single one of my baby boomer clients, and I haven't lost yet. Why? There are two reasons: cash and credit cards.

If you're a typical baby boomer, at least 20 percent of your income is eaten up in credit-card purchases and unrecorded cash expenditures. Whenever you want to buy something and you don't have enough cash in your pocket, you hand the salesperson one of your credit cards. Then, as soon as you leave the store, you head over to the nearest automated teller machine and withdraw some spending money. Maybe it's not a lot of money, but over the weeks and months these purchases and cash withdrawals add up without your even being aware of them.

I think it's this lack of awareness rather than some generational obsession with materialism that accounts for a great deal of baby boomer overspending. Most people are intelligent, mature individuals who, when confronted with the facts, will make the right spending decisions. My goal, therefore, isn't to tell you where you should be spending and where you shouldn't; it's to provide you with the knowledge you need to make those choices wisely.

In order to understand the choices you're making when you spend money, keep track of every penny you spend for three or four months. (Since many bills come due quarterly, you need to do this for at least three months in order to get an accurate measure. A fourth month will just make the result even more accurate.) Buy yourself a little notebook that fits in your pocket and clip a pen to its cover. Every time you spend money, regardless of how much it is or what it's for, write it down on your little pad. At the end of every month categorize your purchases using the worksheet (table 1), total up the numbers, and compare it with your income. The simple fact that you're forced to record each and every purchase will go a long way toward making your spending a conscious rather than reflexive act. The next step is to move from just being conscious of your spending to being thoughtful about it.

Step #2: No Pain, No Gain

One reason many boomers never think about their spending is that with the help of the financial services industry the process has been made almost painless. There's something magical about handing a salesclerk a piece of plastic and receiving merchandise in return. And being able to stick a piece of plastic into a machine and receive cash is absolutely miraculous. It's time to bring the spending process back down to earth.

Open your wallet and remove every single credit or charge card. Take your cash-machine card out as well. Don't worry, I'm not going to leave you penniless. Instead of all that plastic, start carrying your checkbook around with you. When you need to make a purchase, write a check for it. If the merchant doesn't take checks, go to your bank and cash a check for the exact amount you need.

What's the point of all this wallet manipulation? Writing a check takes time. The process forces you to physically subtract the amount of your purchase from your account balance. The time involved gives you a chance to think over each purchase. You'll now have an opportunity to weigh the importance of whatever it is you're buying. The obvious decrease you see in your net worth when you do the arithmetic in your checkbook register forces you to compare this check with others you'll need to write—like the one for your rent or mortgage payment, the one for your daughter's dental visit, the one for your life insurance premium—I'm sure you get the picture.

Similarly, get out of the habit of making shopping a fun activity. Don't shop unless you have a specific purchase in mind. Browsing through a store for fun is a nonsense luxury. When you do go shopping, don't go into a store—any store—without a list of what you need to buy. And never buy anything that isn't on the list regardless of how attractive or inexpensive it may seem. If the item is truly worth buying, add it to the next day's list. This gives you an opportunity to think over the purchase outside the shopping environment. Don't pay any attention to salesclerk claims that "it might not be here tomorrow." They're just reinforcing the need to take one more step in the program and realize that . . .

Step #3: It's a War Out There

Your wallet, not the Kuwaiti desert, is the scene of the greatest war of the 1990s. Every product seller and service provider is fighting to get your money. In addition to fighting among themselves—saying they're better than the competition—they're covertly fighting with you—saying you *need* to spend your money on them. Your grandparents knew this. Your parents were taught this. But if you're like most of my baby boomer clients, up until now you probably haven't been prepared for it. Don't worry, it's not a tough subject to master.

Much of my writing has been on how people can become savvy spenders. All my research and work in this area has led me to the conclusion that there are three basic elements to being a savvy consumer: repairing, planning, and negotiating. Repairing refers to fixing your possessions rather than purchasing a replacement. Planning means thoroughly investigating and researching your alternatives before making a purchase. And negotiating involves taking an active role in the purchase itself; in effect, buying rather than being sold. Let's go over these three elements one by one.

❖ *Repairing.* When was the last time you actually wore something out? Your goal should be to use your possessions for as long as you possibly can. It almost always makes financial sense to spend money on repairing something you already own rather than making another purchase. By spending $65 and repairing your VCR when it breaks down, you'll be spending less than you would in replacing it with a new VCR. And since your prime concern should always be your stream of income, the repair makes financial sense. Be aware of the attacks on this logic, however. Everyone, from the salesperson in the store to your ten-year-old daughter, will be encouraging you to buy a new VCR rather than repair the old one. Just because something isn't state of the art doesn't mean it needs replacing. Unless the repairs will cost you more than the price of a replacement, fix it. Every argument in favor of the replacement purchase focuses on wants, not needs, and emotions, not dollars.

❖ *Planning.* If you're buying something you've never previously owned or if repair doesn't make financial sense, the next element in being a savvy consumer is to plan your purchase. You need to acquire a thorough understanding and knowledge of whatever it is you're about to buy. Then you need to determine which product or service offered best suits your needs and wallet. Finally, you need to determine when you should make the purchase. The Bible says, "To everything there is a season," and that holds for spending, too. Every product and service has a slow period of the year when prices drop or a clearance period when old merchandise must be moved to make way for new.

This research is like a suit of armor protecting you from the attacks of the seller. And it's probably the most readily available suit of armor you'll ever find. Regardless of what it is you're about to buy, there's an article written about it in one or more magazines. High-tech consumer products are reviewed in "buff" publications, such as *MacUser*, *Stereo Review*, and *Popular Photography*. Autos are discussed in periodicals like *Car & Driver*. And whatever these specialty magazines don't cover, *Consumer Reports* does. In it you can find reviews of everything from laundry detergent to life insurance. These reviews can also offer you advice on when is the best time of year to buy. All you need do is head over to your local public library, consult a magazine index, and ask the friendly librarian to bring you the relevant articles. It will cost you nothing but time and could save you hundreds of dollars.

❖ *Negotiating.* The third element in being a savvy consumer, negotiating, will save you even more money than planning. By negotiating I don't necessarily mean haggling over prices, though that can be part of it. I'm referring to taking an active role in the transaction and making sure you're making the decisions and not letting the salesperson make them for you. That could mean comparison shopping, either in person or over the telephone; ordering from a discount catalog rather than buying at a retail store; and bargaining over the price tag.

(Rather than going into great detail about how to negotiate various purchases and transactions, I suggest you take a look at a book I've written on the subject called *The Total Negotiator*. It offers strategies and tactics for nearly every transaction you're likely to face.)

Many of my clients initially think that such measures are time-consuming, old-fashioned, or needlessly frugal. Well, time-consuming and old-fashioned they may be, but needlessly frugal they're not. Your need for frugality is much greater than your parents' need for it was. Your income simply isn't keeping pace with your expenses. If you need a consumer model for your behavior, it would be more accurate to look back to your grandparents, who had to cope with the Great Depression. In fact, that's not a bad credo for the whole spending process: When in doubt, imitate your grandparents.

Savvy Spending Tips

Rather than leave you with the task of quizzing your grandparents on how they made all their spending decisions, I thought I'd give you a head start and offer some specific tips on a handful of expenses, both major and minor.

Doctors and Prescriptions

The secret to savvy spending on doctors and prescriptions is to have the guts to open your mouth and ask questions. There's nothing wrong with asking a doctor how much he or she charges for a checkup, consultation, or procedure, then checking with your insurer as to what is the typical charge for your region. I'm not suggesting that you comparison shop for a physician, but I don't think there's anything wrong with putting your doctor on notice that you care about costs and want to be made aware of them. Similarly, every time your doctor prescribes a medication, ask him not to check the "dispense as written" box, so that the pharmacist can select the most economical option. Then comparison-shop for the cheapest pharmacy.

The best way to save money on medical bills is to take care of yourself: Stop smoking, lose weight if you need to, get a proper amount of rest, eat well, and exercise regularly.

Consumer Electronics

The secret to wise spending on consumer electronics is to realize that since the state of the art changes daily, there's no sense in buying cutting-edge technology. By the time you've learned how to operate your new high-tech equipment, it will no longer be cutting-edge. Instead, spend based on your needs and budget.

When buying an audio system, spend the bulk of your money on speakers—they make the biggest difference in sound quality. Don't fall into the ego trap of buying an amplifier or receiver that's more powerful than necessary. Get enough power to run your speakers efficiently and no more. CD players are all similar electronically but can be very different mechanically. The electronics govern the sound quality, while the mechanics govern the features and generally the cost. Therefore select the unit with only the basic features you need.

When buying a video system, opt for a VCR that's easy to

operate rather than one with a host of complex features. It's amazing how many people to this day still can't program their units properly. If you're in the market for a new television, opt for picture quality as opposed to picture size. Most projection sets produce huge but grainy pictures. I think they're more for your ego than your eyes.

Before you buy an expensive camera, consider your previous photographic experiences. An expensive camera and a set of lenses aren't going to turn you into an avid shutterbug if you've been a "snap shooter" all your life. If you take the occasional snapshot on vacations and family events, opt for the smallest, lightest, easiest-to-use, auto-focus lens-shutter camera you can find, rather than a single lens reflex.

Home Appliances

Don't fall for the allure of buying restaurant-quality appliances. If you're anything like my clients, you spend less time in the kitchen than ever before, since you (and probably your partner) are working long hours. Then why, for goodness' sake, should you buy state-of-the-art refrigerators, stoves, and ovens? Buy what you need, not what you think looks good or what's chic.

When buying washers and dryers, opt for larger, simpler, sturdier units. The fewer buttons, cycles, and features an appliance has the less chance it has to break down. Even if there are only two of you, it makes more economic and environmental sense to buy large-capacity models and use them less frequently. One last note: If you have a choice, opt for a gas appliance. It may cost more initially, but it will pay off in lower utility costs.

Automobiles

Driving has nothing to do with sexual prowess or sensuality. It has nothing to do with status or wealth. Yet many individuals have become obsessed with their cars. The young male boomer may have lusted after a speedy Camaro or Corvette, perhaps to show that his testosterone level was high. As he got a little older, he craved a BMW, I guess to demonstrate that he was rich, tasteful, but still potent. Today he dreams of a Range Rover to show that despite his having a family and some gray on his temples, he's still a rugged individualist, capable of tackling the frontier. This is sheer lunacy.

A car is transportation. No more and no less. You should spend your money on the most economical, safe, and comfortable vehicle you can afford, period. If that's a used vehicle, so be it. Appearance is meaningless. Anyone who judges you by the car you drive isn't someone whose judgment you should value. Performance is generally immaterial. How often do you need to go from zero to sixty miles per hour in eight seconds? And all-terrain capability is often unnecessary. If you live in a snowy climate, you may need four-wheel drive to get around safely, but how often do you need to drive up a cliff or through a swamp?

Make sure to investigate insurance rates and factor that into your buying decisions.

Vacations, Hotels, and Air Fares

There's no rule that says a vacation has to involve a long trip. You can have just as enjoyable or relaxing a time camping two hours from your home as you can staying in a luxury hotel ten hours away. In fact, you could even have a good time just staying put and enjoying your own home and its environs.

Hotels are a place to use the bathroom and sleep, and that's how you should make your spending decisions on accommodations. You aren't traveling to spend time in the room or the lobby, whether you're on a business or pleasure trip, so why spend more than you must? Luxury hotels are for those whose wallets are bottomless or whose egos are fragile.

The same is true of first-class air fare. Sure, on long trips I'm envious of the leg room in the first-class cabin. But the envy subsides a bit when I realize that the only people sitting up there are those who aren't paying for their own ticket or who don't worry what anything costs. Buy airline tickets well in advance, fly mid-week, and stay over weekends and you'll get the best fares. Consider joining frequent-flier clubs that offer discounts on air fares.

Real Estate

I could write a book about spending money on real estate. In fact, I have. It's called *The Field Guide to Home Buying in America*. Rather than get into the whole process, let me simply say that I believe you should spend money only on real estate you intend to use yourself. Don't buy rental properties as an income-generating scheme. By all means, buy a home you intend to live in full-time, a second home you intend to use for vacations or weekends, or even a piece of land you intend to build your dream retirement home on. But don't buy land or buildings as an investment. Leave that to the professionals.

Computers

I'm surprised by the number of my baby boomer clients who are interested in buying computers. When I ask them why, the most common response is "It has become a necessity today." Then when I ask them what they intend to do with their computers, they generally tell me about how they'll track their checkbook, pay their bills, write letters, and play educational games with their children. For a while I thought I must be missing something. Haven't my clients been able to do these things just fine without a computer? Why would they want to go through the entire process of learning how to use their hardware and software just to do things they were already accomplishing with inexpensive tools they knew how to use, like a pencil and paper?

What I was missing was the natural attraction to the latest

technology. When that attraction costs you only a few bucks, I'm not going to waste time and space discussing it. But when it can cost thousands of dollars, as it can with a personal computer, it's my responsibility to raise a warning flag. I think the only justification for owning a personal computer is if you are going to do work at home or if you have a young child for whom the equipment could serve an educational purpose. Otherwise, there's no worthwhile reason for buying one. If you've been successfully balancing your checkbook by hand, continue to do so. If you haven't been able to balance it, no computer is going to help. And if you want to play computer games, go to the nearest arcade with a roll of quarters—you'll spend less in the long run.

Funerals

I know this isn't the most pleasant topic in the world, but it's something you'll need to face up to. Your parents may be living longer than they ever thought possible, but they're still not immortal. And despite all your attention to diet, health, and fitness, neither are you and your mate. That means you'll probably be forced to deal with paying for and arranging funerals. I'll get into this in more detail in chapter 7, but for now let me just say that the secret to doing this wisely is to make the arrangements, or at least decisions, in advance of the need. The worst person to arrange for a funeral is a mourner. Guilt, love, and grief cloud financial judgment. And make no mistake about it, this is a substantial expense that could run up to $4,000. Speak with your parents now and get their feelings on the matter. Have them write down their wishes. If they're up to it, have them make the arrangements. I don't, however, recommend prepaying.

Weddings

It may seem strange moving from funerals to weddings, but they're similar in a lot of ways. They are ritualized, public ceremonies that often involve issues of status, image, and class. And they are both often extraordinarily expensive. I'm not about to debate the merits of a magnificent formal wedding banquet versus a simple ceremony and a potluck dinner. Let me just offer a few words of advice

Always start with a budget. Make sure there is total communication between everyone involved, from family to friends to service providers. The best ways to save time and money are to have the affair on an off-day during an off-season; to have it at a hotel and let the banquet manager put together a package that suits your tastes and budget; or to hire a party adviser who, for a fee, will make all the arrangements for a "custom" affair. Just make sure they're translating your tastes and not foisting their own on you. As with funeral directors, the moment a wedding vendor says, "We never . . . ," or, "We always . . . ," dump them.

Politically Correct Spending

You should never buy something simply because the manufacturer or retailer is a good citizen who contributes a percentage of profits to peace, the rain forest, or the environment. If that product is the best fit for your needs, by all means purchase it. If two products are equal, feel free to opt for the politically correct one. But don't buy a product just because you like the politics of the individual or organization that's selling it. There's nothing wrong with putting your money where your conscience is. It just makes more sense to give directly to peace, the rain forest, or the environment rather than indirectly through a business.

Auto Repairs

People often forget that auto repairs involve two stages: First, the problem needs to be diagnosed, and then it needs to be cured. If you are able to make the diagnosis yourself, you'll be able to save money by bringing the car to a specialist for the repair. For example, you know when you need an oil change or tune-up or have a flat tire or when your muffler falls off or you're having transmission trouble. It will cost you less in those instances to bring the car to the relevant specialist than to a service station or auto dealer. However, if you don't know what's wrong with the car, you'll need the diagnostic skills of a mechanic and will have to pay a bit more.

Memberships

There's nothing wrong with spending money on a membership so long as you use if for the purpose intended. If you join a health club to work out or a golf club to play golf, that's fine. Compare different clubs and opt for the one that offers the best facilities for the money. But don't join a club for social reasons or make your decision based on the status of members or the cachet of belonging. (If joining could be to your financial advantage, that's another story.) If you want to meet people, volunteer for a charitable organization or take a course at the local college. Joining a club for socializing is a waste of money. Lifetime memberships at health clubs almost never make sense; join up for one year at most. And make sure you're able to cancel and receive a refund if you move or become unable to use the facilities.

Subscriptions

Many of my baby boomer clients are reflexive subscribers. After finding they like one or two issues of a publication, they instinctively sign up for a subscription. My suggestion is to wait a couple of months and buy copies at the newsstand instead. If you don't finish an issue before the next arrives or find you can't be bothered to go to the newsstand to pick a new copy up, don't subscribe. If you find that you finish reading an issue and can't wait for the next to arrive, subscribe. And when you do, opt for the shortest term at first. That's because many magazines only have a year's worth of article ideas, which they repeat endlessly. Remember: You can also get magazines, newspapers, recordings, and videotapes at your local public library.

Gifts

Many of my boomer clients are under the mistaken assumption that gift spending can only go up and gift lists can only get bigger. I have no illusions about being able to turn the hands of time back to simpler days when gifts were practical or homemade, but I do have three suggestions that could make gift giving less of a financial drain and more meaningful. First, go over your list every year. Just because you gave your cousin's baby a gift for her first birthday doesn't mean you need to keep on giving each year until the kid graduates from Yale. Second, don't worry about increasing how much you spend each year. Set a budget and stick to it. And third: Instead of spending more money, spend more time thinking about what you'll be giving. Think of something personal, offer a gift of your time, or give something you made yourself. If you're from a large family, consider setting up a gift pool in which every member of the family picks a name out of the hat and gives that person their one gift for the holiday—that's what my family does.

Food Shopping

Never enter a supermarket without a shopping list and go as infrequently as possible. These stores are designed to maximize impulse spending, so the fewer times you're there, the less chance you have to be tempted. Clip coupons and use them even if it means switching brands. Compare unit prices; it often makes sense to buy larger sizes. If there's a bulk-food section, consider purchasing all your staples there. Check produce prices; they vary dramatically with seasonal availability. If there's a farmers' market in your area compare its prices to the supermarket's.

Home Improvements

Here's another topic I've written a book about. (It's called *The Big Fix Up.*) But rather than go on for pages, let me give you the one essential message: The only home improvements that make sense are those that add to the value of the home rather than just to your ego or pleasure. Worthwhile renovations include modernizing and updating the building systems (new plumbing, oil burner, roof, windows, etc.); renovating kitchens and bathrooms—within reason; and adding aboveground living space. Luxuries, like swimming pools and finished basements, are, pardon the pun, sunk money.

Gratuities

Ask any waiter or waitress and they'll tell you that baby boomers are among the best tippers in the world. I think this is because many boomers are uncomfortable about having someone, particularly a peer or elder, wait on them like a servant. To compensate for this violation of the egalitarian code they lived by in the 1960s, many boomers overtip. My suggestion is to free yourself from guilt over gratuities. If a service charge is included in the bill, don't give an additional tip. If service has been acceptable, leave 15 percent. If it has been exceptional, leave 20 percent. If it has been terrible and you feel uncomfortable leaving nothing, leave 7–10 percent and tell the manager why you did so. If you just leave the small tip and don't tell anyone why, the waiter or waitress will just assume you're cheap.

Interest and Finance Charges

It generally makes sense to, if possible, pay off credit-card balances you have. The amount of interest charges you're accruing almost certainly outweighs any interest you're earning on the money, so you'll actually be saving money by paying your balances off. Consider increasing your monthly mortgage payments if you can. By increasing your payment by as little as 5 percent, you could shave almost seven years off the mortgage. Finally, try to avoid bank charges, since they're an expense that gains you absolutely nothing.

Transportation

Whenever possible, walk, ride a bicycle, or take public transportation rather than drive. Investigate car pools for both yourself and your children. Speak to your supervisor about changing your work schedule from five 8-hour days to four 10-hour days; you'll cut your cost of commuting by 20 percent.

Entertainment, Dining Out, and Socializing

These are three areas where baby boomers spend an extraordinary amount of money. That's not because they have some proclivity to luxury but because with both partners working long hours just to keep up with the bills, social activities take on increased importance. There are ways to cut down and still have a good time. Have potluck dinners rather than dinner parties. Invite friends over for coffee and dessert rather than a full meal. Rent videos and make your own popcorn rather than going to the movies. If you simply must see a new film before it comes out on videotape, go to a matinee; it may cost half as much. Cook extra-large portions on the weekends and have leftovers during the week rather than grabbing take-out food. Make eating out a special occasion rather than a regular activity. Write letters rather than making long-distance calls and stop screening all your incoming calls. If you screen calls and then call people back when you're in the mood, you'll have to pay for the call; pick up the phone and it's on their bill.

Now that you've secured and maximized the efficiency of your stream of income, your next step is to take measures to protect it from catastrophe.

··

Chapter Six

Insuring Your Stream of Income

Nothing is permanent. Your world can change in the blink of an eye, so you have to be prepared for it.
—Erik Kolbell, *minister for peace and social justice at*
Riverside Church

The fourth step in surviving the squeeze is to insure your stream of income. The single biggest threat to the ability of you and your family to survive the squeeze is a temporary or permanent disruption in your stream of income. Such a disruption could be caused by an illness that leads to massive and unavoidable medical bills; losing your job; a disability that leaves you unable to work; an inability to care for yourself; or death.

People have always faced these potential catastrophes. Since only the wealthy had the financial resources to protect themselves, everyone else used to rely on family, friends, and the community to help them overcome financial disasters. But as the population grew larger, society became more industrialized, and freedom of movement expanded, these informal safety nets could no longer be counted on for financial support. This led to the development of a formal safety net: insurance.

Insurance began in London when a group of shipping merchants were being devastated by the losses of their vessels at sea. Individually they couldn't compensate for these disasters. In an effort to protect themselves, they decided to form a pool.

···

Each merchant would contribute money to the pool, and if he suffered a loss, the pool would compensate him. Since there were so many merchants involved and the odds of them all suffering losses at the same time were infinitesimal, they could contribute less money to the pool than they would have had to set aside to protect themselves. In effect, by spreading the risk among many, they were cutting the cost and making complete protection possible.

Obviously, the idea worked. Insurance was soon being applied to all manner of risks. As the pools grew larger, they needed full-time management, since money that's unmanaged shrinks in value. That led to the development of insurance companies that would take the pool of money and invest it to make sure it retained its value. Like all other businesses, these insurance companies were primarily concerned with maintaining their existence and growing. In order to do that, they needed more funds. To get those funds, insurance companies began offering the members of their pools investment returns as well as protection from disaster. Since the business of investing offered more dramatic (if less certain) profits than the business of simply insuring, insurance companies have moved further and further away from their original purpose and entered the financial-services field. They've tried to complicate their insurance products by turning them into investments.

While pure insurance may not be very profitable and desirable for insurance companies, it's still a wonderful tool for individuals. Insurance is the single best defense against disruptions in your stream of income and therefore a vital step in surviving the squeeze. Baby boomers need to find the closest thing to pure insurance available that can protect them from each of the threats to their stream of income. And when none is available, they'll need to protect themselves. Let's examine each threat individually and see how you can best protect yourself and your dependents. I'll go over them in the order of their probability of occurring, which is the order in which they should be addressed.

Illness Leading to Massive Medical Bills

While an illness may not cause your stream of income to dry up, it can be a tremendous drain on your resources. The costs of medical care are so high that even if a member of your family needs to be hospitalized, it can throw you into a financial tailspin. That's why health insurance has become a common employee benefit. But that's not much comfort to entrepreneurs or to those whose employers don't offer health insurance. If you're forced to purchase your own health insurance, you'll face a dizzying number of choices and options, none of which are clearcut. The only thing that's certain about health insurance is that it's very expensive. While there are many variables, you can expect to pay around $4,000 a year for decent family coverage.

There are three primary types of health insurance: hospitalization, major medical, and dental. These can be purchased separately or together in a package. Hospitalization covers doctors' and nurses' bills while you're in the hospital; surgery in and out of the hospital; room-and-board charges for a bed in a semiprivate room or an intensive care unit; and other hospital services, including lab tests, X-rays, and prescriptions. Major medical covers nonsurgical treatment by a physician outside a hospital. Depending on the policy, visits to chiropractors and various types of therapists may also be covered. Dental covers noncosmetic dental treatment. Orthodontia is generally not covered.

Even with Health Insurance Coverage You'll Still Have to Pay

Having health insurance doesn't mean you won't pay for your treatment. Most policies require you to pay for a certain amount of care yourself, before benefits kick in. This payment is called a deductible and can range anywhere from $100 to $1,000, either per person or per family. It's often possible to choose your own deductible. The higher a deductible you select, the lower your premium will be.

After meeting your deductible, you still might have to pay part of the cost of care, generally either 20 or 25 percent, through what's called coinsurance. The more you pay in coinsurance, the lower your premiums. Often the requirement to pay coinsurance is waived after bills reach a certain point in any one year. At that point, the insurance company will pay 100 percent of the cost. But even if you reach that point, you might still have bills to pay.

Insurance companies base their benefits not on what your doctor or hospital charges but on what they deem to be "reasonable and customary" charges. If your doctor charges more than the insurance company thinks he should, you'll have to pick up the extra cost. In addition, there are some services for which insurance companies will pay only a specific amount or percentage. For example, many insurers will cover visits to a psychotherapist but will either pay only a set amount, such as $20 per visit, or a set percentage, such as 50 percent of the bill.

Finally, insurance companies limit the amount of money they will pay out in benefits either per year, per illness, or per lifetime. For example, some policies will pay out no more than $250,000 in lifetime benefits, though $1 million is a more common limit. Others will pay out no more than $25,000 for hospitalization in any one year, or no more than $10,000 per illness. The lower the limits on benefits, the lower your premium will be.

Things to Watch Out for When Purchasing Health Insurance

When you're shopping around for health insurance coverage there are a few nuances in policies that you should look out for:

- Make sure your policy is guaranteed renewable. Otherwise, you can be dropped if you develop a serious illness or your bills reach a certain level. And once you're dropped, it's very difficult to obtain replacement coverage.
- Check to see if there's an initial waiting period before the policy actually begins providing benefits.

- Find out the insurer's policy on preexisting conditions. Some require you to wait twelve to eighteen months for coverage on any preexisting condition. Others refuse to cover them at all.
- Some hospitalization policies won't pay benefits for procedures done on your first day in a hospital. Make sure your coverage starts immediately upon being admitted.
- There are hospitalization policies that will pay for services only at an "approved" hospital. Make sure the hospitals you're likely to use are approved by the insurance company.
- Many policies require second opinions and preapprovals prior to nonemergency surgical procedures, sometimes even requiring that an "approved physician" render the second opinion. Make sure your policy allows you or your physician to select a doctor for a second opinion and that you follow any preapproval rules to the letter.
- Check to see if the policy automatically increases benefits to keep pace with inflation. If not, your out-of-pocket costs could rise dramatically each year.
- Investigate whether or not a newborn is automatically covered under your existing policy and how long a child is covered. Some policies stop covering all children at age eighteen. Others continue to provide coverage until age twenty-one, as long as a child is in college.
- Better policies will have a provision that waives your premium if you become disabled.

Cutting Your Health Insurance Costs

There are really only three ways to cut your health insurance costs and still obtain adequate coverage: You can join together with others and buy a group policy, you can become as much of a self-insurer as possible, or you can join a managed-care organization.

Group policies are almost always more affordable than individual policies simply because they spread the risks and costs among many people. Many business organizations and professional associations offer group health coverage to their members. In fact, there are quite a few such associations whose sole purpose is to serve as a health insurance group. You may have to pay annual dues to join these groups, but generally you'll more than recoup the cost in reduced health insurance premiums.

Remember: Your goal in taking out health insurance is to protect yourself from catastrophic, not routine, medical bills. You can dramatically lower your costs by absorbing as much of the cost of routine care as you can—in effect, becoming a self-insurer. There are two ways you can do this. First, you can take the highest deductible and coinsurance percentage available. And second, you can make sure your coverage is cost-effective. For example, the cost of dental insurance is often the same as, or even greater than, the cost of two yearly checkups. If your teeth are relatively healthy, it may make sense to absorb the risk of big dental bills yourself rather than paying an insurance company to take it on.

Managed-care organizations are insurance companies and medical-care providers combined. There are three primary types: health maintenance organizations (HMOs), health insurance providers (HIPs), and preferred provider organizations (PPOs). These are either loose confederations of doctors or clinics; they lower costs by, in effect, reducing your choices of health-care providers. Generally there are no deductibles, no forms to fill out, and only a minor coinsurance payment of anywhere from $5 to $10 per visit. There are some things you should be aware of, however. First, your relationship with your personal physician may not be very personal. Second, you may have to wait longer for nonemergency appointments than you would with a traditional physician. And third, it's important that the group is affiliated with a high-quality hospital—many aren't.

These managed-care organizations are the wave of the future, and many provide excellent care. However, make it your business to investigate any such organization before committing to it.

If You're Covered by Your Employer

Before I leave the topic of health insurance, there are two things I want to point out to those who are covered by an employer:

If you find that your existing plan isn't sufficient in the first place or is being trimmed by a cost-conscious employer, you can buy a supplemental policy to cover any gaps in coverage. Just make sure to check with your current insurer first. Insurance companies often offer special rates to existing policyholders that are much lower than you're likely to find elsewhere.

If both you and your spouse are covered by health insurance from your jobs, make sure to file claims with both companies. While you can't claim more than 100 percent of your costs—that would be fraud—a secondary insurer will pick up the cost of your coinsurance. For example, if you've met your deductible and have a doctor's bill for $200, your insurer will pay 80 percent, or $160. If you then submit the same claim to your spouse's insurance company, it will pay the remaining 20 percent, or $40.

Loss of Job

As I mentioned back in chapters 3 and 4, there's no such thing as job security anymore. Your security lies in your ability to use and market your individual skills, not your current job or business. While I've tried to give you the tools to deal with, and in fact benefit from, this new environment, I'd be misleading you if I said you'd *never* have to deal with being fired.

While insurance companies see no profit in providing unemployment insurance for individuals, there's obviously still a need for it. As in many cases where the profits are low or nil for business but the need is great, government has stepped in to fill the gap. The massive joblessness during the Great Depression led to the creation of mandatory unemployment insurance for full-time employees. Money is deducted from each of your paychecks and put into a pool that can then be drawn on when you're out of work. But while it's a noble gesture on the part of government, it falls far short of providing actual protection.

Unemployment insurance benefits vary from state to state, but uniformly they are meager and temporary. As with most government insurance programs the idea is to pay a subsistence benefit that will keep the recipient from being totally impoverished through loss of employment but at the same time encourage the individual to find another job as soon as possible. Sometimes, when the job market is very tough, the benefit period is extended. However, the amount of benefits remains too low even to pay rent in most places. In New York City, for example, where most of my clients live, the benefits will just about pay for their travel expenses to look for another job. Other government benefit programs—such as food stamps and Medicaid—all depend on your being truly impoverished. That leaves you with only one option: You have to protect yourself. And the only way to do that is to establish a cash reserve—your own pool of money that can be drawn on in case you temporarily lose your stream of income.

Establishing a Cash Reserve

How much of a reserve do you need? I tell my employee-clients to set aside enough money to pay their expenses for six months. In the previous chapter I encouraged you to keep track of, and categorize, every penny you spent for three or four months. That should tell you what your monthly expenses actually are. I realize you may be out of work for more than six months, but if you go on an austerity budget, factor in your severance pay and your unemployment insurance benefits, and approach family and friends for help if need be, this cushion can be made to stretch for as long as nine months or a year without a stream of income. If you're still unemployed after that length of time, you'll have to either begin selling some assets, change your lifestyle dramatically, or take any job that's available.

Where do you come up with this money if you don't already have it? Once again, go back to chapter 5. By becoming aware of your spending, you've begun to spend less. Those savings can serve as the seeds of this cash reserve. If you haven't yet come up with any savings, eliminate some of your spending on nonnecessities. For example, I tell my clients to entirely give up dining out, buying new clothes, and taking taxicabs until they've established their cash reserve.

The choice of how much and what you give up is yours alone. All I can do is stress that for your short-term financial stability and your long-term ability to survive the squeeze, you need to have a cash reserve. After health insurance, it's the most important protection for your stream of income.

Investing Your Cash Reserve

Once you've accumulated a cash reserve, don't simply put it all in a bank account. That's the equivalent of hiding it under your mattress. While you want this money to be liquid, you're not going to need it all at once. Assume that you'll be able to live for at least one month by combining your severance, unemployment benefits, and whatever cash you have on hand. Take another two months' worth of your cash reserve and put it in a money market fund so it will be readily available when your cash on hand and severance runs out. The rest can be invested in any number of financial instruments, such as short-term certificates of deposit, government bonds and notes of intermediate duration, or mutual funds that deal with short-term municipal bonds. What matters is that you maximize your return while making sure the maturities of these instruments are staggered so they come due when you need the money. One last point: Make sure to reinvest the interest you receive on your cash reserve. That should ensure that it keeps pace with inflation.

Disability Leaving You Unable to Work

The single biggest financial mistake most of my baby boomer clients make is that they don't carry sufficient disability insurance. Most Americans fail to adequately insure themselves against disability, but in the case of baby boomers, this failure is even more glaring. That's because boomers, as a rule, are more dependent on their streams of income (and their mate's) than their elders and will have less of an opportunity to establish a safety net in the future.

Disability is one of the two potential financial catastrophes that most people forget about. (The other is long-term nursing-home care, which we'll address next.) You probably have auto insurance in case you get into an accident, health insurance in case you get sick, homeowner's insurance in case your house burns down, and life insurance in case you die from these or any other calamity. Yet without adequate disability insurance you have no protection in case a sickness, car accident, fire, or other disaster causes you to be unable to work. Between the ages of thirty-five and sixty, you have a four times greater chance of becoming disabled than of dying. And with medicine constantly improving, making it more likely you'll survive catastrophic diseases and injuries, the odds of becoming disabled rather than dying will continue to rise.

Your family's financial life and your ability to survive the squeeze are hostage to your ability to continue to work and generate a stream of income. If you can't work and your stream of income dries up, all your other plans will crumble. I know this from personal experience.

At the age of forty-eight I was diagnosed as having tuberculosis. I lost my job (I was a banker at the time) and was unable to work for two years. At the time, two of my children were in college, and two were in high school. My wife had only recently reentered the job market. We were living well but had almost no safety net. The only thing that saved me financially was my disability insurance. If this book does nothing else, I'll consider it successful if it persuades you to take out adequate disability coverage.

Your Present Disability Coverage Is Probably Inadequate

When I explain the need for disability insurance to my baby boomer clients, their first response is to say they're already covered either through a company or government plan. That's partially true. Most people are covered. They're just not covered adequately.

Workers' compensation insurance varies from state to state, but the maximum benefit is either two-thirds of gross wages or 80 percent of net wages, up to a specified ceiling. Like unemployment insurance, the benefit ceilings are low, since the coverage is designed to keep you from falling into poverty, not to maintain your life-style. In addition, workers' compensation covers only work-related injuries.

Most companies and unions have their own disability plans. Generally they pay benefits of from 40 to 60 percent of net wages for from three months to a year. Not only is this too little for too short a period of time; it also stays in effect only while you are employed by the provider. When you leave your job—and as we know, you will be leaving jobs often in the future—you lose the coverage. And when you get another job, you may not qualify for disability coverage right away. Entrepreneurs, of course, won't have any coverage from employers or unions.

Social Security does have a disability benefit. But it's extremely difficult to obtain. First, either you or your spouse must have worked long enough to qualify. Second, you must be so disabled that you can't work in *any* substantial job. Third, it must be expected that your disability will last at least a year or will lead to your death. And fourth, even if you pass the other conditions, checks won't start arriving until you've been disabled for five consecutive months. These conditions are strictly enforced to prevent fraud. More than two-thirds of applicants are turned down.

The government also offers disability coverage to military veterans, but only if the disability can be traced to something that happened when they were on active duty. Only totally disabled, low-income veterans can obtain benefits for disabilities that aren't related to military service, but even they must have served in wartime.

Some states and possessions, including California, Hawaii, New Jersey, New York, Rhode Island, and Puerto Rico, offer disability, but the benefits usually run for a limited number of weeks.

Disability Coverage Is Expensive, but It's Necessary

After I detail why their present coverage is likely to be inadequate, many baby boomer clients raise a second objection: Disability policies are expensive. Again, that's a partial truth. Disability insurance is expensive, but it's still necessary. In fact, the reason it's so expensive is that it's so often used.

For a thirty-five-year-old man who earns $50,000 to obtain 60 percent coverage through the age of sixty-five, he'll have to pay $1,110 a year. If he wants benefits to last his entire lifetime, he'll have to pay $1,164. And costs are only going to get higher. There are more and more claims being made for drug abuse, stress-related diseases, pregnancy, and exercise-related injuries. And once again, medical advances will lead to more disabled survivors of catastrophic diseases.

Since premiums are lower the younger you are, since costs are only going to get higher across the board, and since it's an essential step in surviving the squeeze, the only answer is to take out an adequate policy as soon as possible. And if you make some savvy compromises in selecting your coverage, the financial sting can be reduced.

Before I get into those possible compromises, I want to add three bits of advice: First, be wary of group policies offered by professional associations and trade groups. While the premiums are often lower than on individual policies, they may not provide you with the coverage you need. Second, if you're thinking of going into business for yourself, take out disability coverage before you leave your present job. Insurers ask for a tremendous amount of income documentation. As an entrepreneur, you'll spend most of your time on tax avoidance, making it difficult to prove your "real" income. And third, if you're part of a two-income household that relies on both incomes, make sure both you and your mate take out disability insurance.

Calculating How Much Disability Coverage You'll Need

The natural inclination is to take out enough disability insurance to replace your current income. But the higher the benefits you want, the higher your premium will be. The first compromise, then, is to buy the coverage you need, not want. Let me explain:

If you are paying the premiums on a disability policy, the benefits are tax-free. If someone else, such as an employer, is paying the premiums, the income is taxable. (Worker's compensation benefits generally aren't taxable. State benefits aren't taxable unless they're made in lieu of unemployment insurance, which is taxable. Up to half of Social Security disability benefits may be taxable, depending on how much other income you're receiving.) That means that when you're taking your own coverage, you should begin with your net rather than gross income.

If you're disabled, some of your expenses will decrease. For example, since you're not working, you won't be commuting, eating lunch out, buying new suits, or going to the dry cleaner as often. Some of your personal expenses, such as entertainment and travel, may be less as well. That means you'll actually need less income.

If your mate isn't working full-time now, he may be able to pick up the slack and bring in extra dollars. The same is true for older children. Their potentially increased contributions can translate into lower benefits and therefore lower premiums.

Insurers won't knowingly sell you enough insurance to cover your entire income, anyway, since they feel that destroys your incentive to return to work. Most middle-income people will be able to obtain coverage for only 60–70 percent of their income. High-income people may be able to get only 30–55 percent.

Deciding How Quickly Disability Payments Should Start

The longer it takes for payments to start after you become disabled, the lower your premiums will be. That's because since most disabilities are temporary, the longer the delay in payments, the less the insurer will probably have to pay out in total. A 180-day wait for benefits could cut your premiums by 30 percent. Therefore, your second compromise should be pushing the first payment as far into the future as possible.

Take a look at the timing of your other disability policies. When does your coverage through work begin and end? When will state and federal plans start, and how long will they last? Add the cash reserves you've set aside for loss of job into the equation. How long will that money last? Your goal is to have benefits from the policy you're buying kick in only after all your other substantial benefits and reserves have run out, therefore lowering your premium.

For example: If your employer's disability plan starts paying benefits four weeks after you've become disabled and then continues to pay for three months and you have a cash reserve of three months, you'll be able to buy a policy that starts paying benefits after six months. For the first month you're disabled you'll be able to live off your savings. Then, for the next three months, you'll be able to live off the benefits from your employer's plan. When that runs out, you'll be able to use your savings for another two months. At that point you'll need the benefits from your own policy to start.

Estimating How Long Disability Payments Should Last

The next area of possible compromise is how long your benefits will last. Once again, since they want you to return to work as soon as possible, insurers try to limit the duration of payments. The longer benefits last, the higher your premium will be. But you have to be very careful about making compromises here.

Most disabilities (90 percent) last less than two years, and policies that pay benefits for only a year or two are very affordable. However, if you take out one of these policies and you're one of the 10 percent of disabled individuals who are out of work for more than two years, you'll only have delayed the disaster.

My suggestion is to obtain enough coverage to last at least until you're age sixty-five, not because you would have stopped working then anyway, but because at that point you'll qualify for Social Security retirement benefits and perhaps pension payments. Lifetime benefits are available, but they can be very expensive.

Deciding How Disability Should Be Defined

The final area for compromise is in how your policy will define disability. This is another place where care is important. Every policy has its own definition of disability. Most of them are artfully written to limit the insurer's responsibility as much as possible. You could be an attorney earning $250,000 a year who suffers a severe head injury, making it impossible to practice law. But if your policy has a very narrow definition of disability, the insurance company may refuse to pay benefits if you could conceivably work at, say, McDonald's.

That's what leads many people to take out what's called "own occupation" coverage. However, this is the most expensive option. And since your major concern is your income, not your occupation, I suggest you opt for the lower-priced "income replacement" coverage. Under this definition you are disabled if your income drops due to an illness or injury.

Types of Disability Policies

With the standard disability policy you pay the same annual premium for as long as the policy is in effect. While the risk of disability is greater the older you get, the insurer spreads out the premiums evenly. In effect, you'll be overpaying early on and underpaying later. While I recommend that you buy a standard policy if you can afford it, there are some other types of policies available that could make it easier for you to afford adequate coverage right away.

Step rate policies offer low initial premiums but then increase them dramatically each year. While they're the cheapest policy initially, the steps may be too big for your income to keep pace with. A better option, I believe, is an *annually renewable policy*. These have a slightly higher initial premium, but the yearly increases are lower than those of step rate policies and more in line with the rate your income is likely to increase. By taking out an annually renewable policy, you may be able to save 25–50 percent off your initial cost. The downside, however, is that as you grow older, the premiums will be astronomical. If the only way you can afford disability coverage now is to take out an annually renewable policy, then do so. But I urge you to switch to a standard policy as soon as you possibly can.

Examining Disability Policies

Disability policies are very complex documents requiring careful examination. Here are some things to look for:

❖ *In what class does the policy put your profession?* Insurance companies categorize professions by the likelihood of injury and the likelihood of someone in them wanting to return to work as soon as possible. The cheapest rates are given to those in Class Five professions: accountants, attorneys, architects, college professors, dentists, doctors, and pharmacists. The next-lowest rates are given to those in Class Four professions: technicians, office workers, and other professionals. Since different insurance companies categorize professions differently, look for a policy that puts you in the best class possible.

❖ *Are waiting periods standardized?* Make sure the policy doesn't have one waiting period for disabilities that come from illness and another for those that come from injury. Your need for benefits won't change because of how or why you've become disabled.

119

Homeowner's Insurance

While homeowner's insurance doesn't protect your stream of income, it does secure your most valuable asset and so deserves some attention. Here are some tips to make sure you have adequate and efficient coverage:

• Take the highest deductible you can afford to reduce your premium. This is protection from catastrophes like fires, not broken windows.

• Cover your home for replacement value—how much it will cost to be rebuilt—rather than market (resale) value.

• Make sure replacement value is adjusted regularly to account for inflation and doesn't include the value of the land, which can't burn up.

• Buy an HO3 category policy, which covers the structure and personal property from damage due to all hazards except floods, earthquakes, sewer backups, and wars.

• If you're at high risk from floods and earthquakes, you'll need to purchase separate, specialized policies.

• Personal property is generally insured up to 50 percent of the face value of the policy and at market value (flea market cost less depreciation), not replacement cost. Replacement-value coverage is desirable but costs more.

• Valuables, such as jewelry, silver, and furs, are covered only for a set amount. You can take out additional coverage for each item, but make sure the items are truly replaceable and that you would actually want to replace them. You may not be able to, or even want to, replace a lost heirloom, for example. Valuables that are irreplaceable should be kept in safety deposit boxes when not in use.

• You may be able to lower your premiums by installing dead-bolt locks, smoke detectors, fire extinguishers, and/or burglar alarms.

Auto Insurance

The insurance on your automobile(s) is probably one of your biggest expenses, and it's one you may have very little control over, since rates are somewhat determined by where you live and coverage levels are often mandated by states. There are a few things you can do to lower your premiums:

• Drop collision coverage on cars that are over three years old, since they've depreciated so much in value that they may not be worth repairing.

• Drop comprehensive coverage if your homeowner's policy covers property stolen from your car.

• Drop towing coverage if you belong to an auto club that offers road service.

• Take the highest deductible you can afford; that will lower your premium dramatically.

• Reduce the amount of miles you drive annually and your rates may go down.

• If you take a defensive driving course, you'll receive a lower rate. You can take these courses every twelve to eighteen months.

• Carefully analyze the selection of who will be considered the primary driver of each vehicle.

❖ *What is the renewability option?* There are three types: class cancelable, which allow the insurer to cancel policies in any given group; guaranteed renewable, which allow the insurer to raise premiums but which cannot be canceled as long as the premiums are paid on time; and guaranteed renewable and noncancelable, which prohibit the insurer from raising premiums or canceling as long as premiums are paid on time.

❖ *What does the policy say about preexisting conditions?* Some policies refuse to cover disabilities resulting from preexisting conditions that you've failed to reveal regardless of how

Have a Home Inventory

The best way to ensure that claims on your homeowner's policy are filed and paid quickly is to have an inventory of your home. This can either be a videotape or a series of photographs, supplemented with a list or voice-over describing every item, including model number, price, and date of purchase. I don't think there's any need to hire a public insurance adjuster to help with the processing of claims. If you have patience and good records, you can do all the paperwork yourself and save the 10–15 percent fee an adjuster charges.

long ago they first occurred, while others won't cover preexisting conditions for only the first one or two years the policy is in effect.

❖ *What are the policy's rules on intermittent disabilities?* Some require you to go through the waiting period for benefits once per calendar year; with others you must go through the waiting period every time you make a claim. Since you've selected a policy with as long a waiting period as possible, you can't afford to go through the waiting period more than once a year.

❖ *What does the policy say about waiver of premiums?* Some policies waive your premiums while you're receiving benefits; others require you to continue paying.

❖ *Does the policy discuss partial disabilities?* If you are partially disabled, you will want to be able to receive partial benefits that are equivalent to your loss in income. Avoid policies that pay benefits only for total disabilities.

❖ *Is rehabilitation covered?* You want a policy that will pay for any and all necessary rehabilitation and therapy so that you can go back to work as soon as possible.

❖ *Are there any exclusions?* Generally, policies will exclude from coverage pregnancy and disabilities resulting from military service. If there are any other exclusions, look for another policy.

Riders to Avoid in a Disability Policy

As with most complex insurance policies, there are some riders you should avoid:

- Some insurers offer a premium refund rider that gives you a refund on premiums paid if you go five or ten years without filing a claim. This rider will increase your premium by at least 50 percent, so I recommend avoiding it.
- Occasionally you'll find a rider that, for a higher premium, offers to pay you an income while you are hospitalized. If you have hospitalization coverage already, this is unnecessary.
- Another common rider is for accidental death and dismemberment. For an additional fee the insurer will pay a benefit if you die or lose a limb in an accident. Accident insurance is nonsense. Your needs don't change depending on how you're disabled or why you die.

Riders to Request in a Disability Policy

There are three riders you should try to have added to your policy if you can afford the increased premium:

❖ *A Social Security replacement rider* adds to your benefit check the amount you would have received in Social Security disability payments if the government turns down your application.

❖ *An option-to-buy rider* guarantees you the right to buy additional coverage in the future, if you pass a physical exam. If you don't want to have to go through a physical again, you'll have to pay a bit more. This is valuable, since at some point your expenses may increase, requiring you to have more coverage.

❖ *A cost-of-living rider* adjusts your benefits for inflation, using some type of economic index. This is also important, for it's the only way to make sure your benefits retain their real value. Just make sure the index that the insurer uses isn't of their own creation. This was a real lifesaver for me when I was collecting disability; and the added cost wasn't that much.

Inability to Care for Yourself

The second gap in protection that most of my baby boomer clients have is the lack of nursing-home insurance. Hospitalization insurance—whether through private insurance when you're young or through Medicare when you're older—covers only recuperative or rehabilitative stays in nursing homes and medically necessary home care. Custodial care, or assistance in carrying out the daily tasks of living, is not covered.

I'll be going over long-term-care insurance, or nursing-home insurance, as it's sometimes called, in great detail in chapter 7, when I address your parents' needs. That's because, since they're older, their need for it is more pressing. But I would be remiss if I didn't point out that it's important for you to investigate this coverage for yourself as well. The cost of this insurance is dramatically lower the earlier it's purchased. It's definitely a risk you need to address: Only one policyholder in a thousand will ever collect on a homeowner's policy, and only one in a hundred will ever collect on an auto insurance policy, but about one in five will collect on a long-term-care policy. And while your parents have the option of having the government pick up the tab through the Medicaid system, in all probability, by the time you're old enough to need nursing-home care, Medicaid will no longer be around.

Death

Of course, everyone who holds a life insurance policy will eventually collect on it—or at least their beneficiaries will. This guarantee of a payout, as well as remarkable salesmanship, has led most Americans to take out life insurance. Nearly all my baby boomer clients have some form of life insurance. The problem is they generally have either too much or the wrong kind. Almost every one of my baby boomer clients is overspending on life insurance, and I'd bet the same is true of you.

The purchase of life insurance should not be an emotional decision. I know it's hard to stay rational about your own death. I've had clients break down and cry in my office when talking about how they want to leave "a legacy" to their children. But if you're going to survive the squeeze, you'll need to abandon all the myths about life insurance you may have picked up over the years.

Life Insurance Myths and Truths

What myths am I talking about? That:

- the amount of life insurance carried is a measure of your worth as a human being;
- the amount of life insurance carried indicates the extent of the insured's love for his beneficiaries;
- life insurance is a replacement for the deceased;
- life insurance is an investment;
- everyone should carry life insurance; and
- life insurance should ensure that beneficiaries "will never have to worry about money."

Life insurance should do two things: (1) pay any outstanding debts of the deceased that would become an unwelcome burden for a survivor and (2) temporarily replace the deceased's stream of income a survivor has sufficient time to make life-style adjustments. That's it. The myths are wrong: Life insurance isn't a sign of love or worth; no amount of money can ever replace a human being; life insurance shouldn't be an investment vehicle; not everyone needs life insurance; and it's both morbid and unrealistic to think your beneficiaries could, or even should, be made wealthy by your death.

If you've no dependents, you don't need life insurance—it's that simple. Since there's no one for your debts to be passed on to, there's no reason for you to take out insurance to pay them off. You can make other arrangements if you don't want your estate to be saddled with bills. Children certainly don't need life insurance, since they have no dependents. However, both spouses in a two-income family may need life insurance policies. In addition, in some situations life insurance could serve a sound business purpose for entrepreneurs without dependents.

How Much Life Insurance Do You Need?

The secret of figuring out exactly how much life insurance you need is to take the two functions of life insurance—payment of debts and temporary income replacement—and assign specific numbers to them.

The first debt you'll need to consider is the cost of your funeral. I'm a firm believer in preplanning funerals as a way to eliminate the overspending that's endemic to them. Make a few telephone calls and get price quotes. Speak to your family and make your wishes clear. Write down what you'd like done. And put a price tag on it.

In addition to covering your funeral costs, you'll want your life insurance to pay off any outstanding debts that would be unwelcome to your survivors. That generally means consumer debts, such as credit cards and auto loans. Don't jump to include mortgage debt in this category. Many of my widowed older clients who reflexively used life insurance benefits to pay off their mortgages regretted the move later on, since it robbed them of a substantial tax deduction. If you know your survivors will want to stay in your current home and you don't think they'll be able to handle the mortgage payments even after adjusting their life-styles, consider setting aside enough life insurance money to pay the mortgage down to an affordable level rather than paying it off entirely. That will at least let them retain part of the mortgage interest deduction.

Steer clear from insurance policies that are specifically designed to pay off your debts, such as mortgage insurance and credit life insurance. These are the worst economic deals around. They are known as decreasing or declining term insurance. With these policies your premium stays the same, while the face value of the policy decreases. For example, you pay $15 every month for mortgage insurance as part of your payment. Each month, however, the amount of money you owe on the mortgage decreases. You're much better off covering your debts with a traditional policy in which the face value remains constant.

Assigning numbers to the second purpose of life insurance, income replacement, is a bit more difficult. It's unrealistic (and extraordinarily expensive) to replace your income for the rest of your beneficiaries' lives. You and they must accept the fact that there must be an adjustment in the family's standard of living at some point; the trick is determining when that point should be. First, you must judge how long it will take your beneficiaries to adjust to your absence. For example, if you and your mate both work and are child-free, it probably won't take her that long to adjust her life-style to the loss of your income. However, if you and your mate have children and you're the only income producer, it could take a great deal of time for your mate to be able to adjust. She may need training prior to entering the job market. And if the children are young, there will be added child-care costs.

Don't forget to assign an insurable value to the work of a stay-at-home spouse. If the stay-at-home spouse in a one-income family with children dies, the surviving spouse will need to arrange and pay for child care and home care—two substantial expenses. In this situation it may make sense to insure for an amount large enough to pay for child and home care until the children are able to take care of themselves and help with the housework.

Remember, your goal isn't to replace your income for the rest of your survivors' lives but to give them a sufficient period

TABLE 2. LIFE-INSURANCE-NEED WORKSHEET

	Income Earner #1	Income Earner #2
1. Cost of preplanned funeral	_____	_____
2. Outstanding credit-card debt	_____	_____
3. Outstanding auto-loan debt	_____	_____
4. Amount needed to pay down mortgage to level affordable for surviving dependents	_____	_____
5. Expense and debt-coverage need (total of lines 1 through 4)	_____	_____
6. Amount needed to replace income or pay for home care for as long as it takes surviving dependents to adjust life-style	_____	_____
7. Social Security benefits	_____	_____
8. Job-related benefits	_____	_____
9. Income replacement need (line 6 minus lines 7 and 8)	_____	_____
10. Life insurance need (line 5 plus line 9)	_____	_____

of time to make needed adjustments. This is an estimation that is unique to every situation and requires everyone in the family to sit down and deal with it rationally.

Before you total up your numbers for funeral costs, debt payments, and life-style adjustments, there's one more number you need to factor in: Social Security survivor's benefits. Your spouse is entitled to Social Security survivor's benefits up to your youngest child's sixteenth birthday. Your children are entitled to survivor's benefits up to age eighteen if they're not in school full-time and age nineteen if they are in school full-time. In order to find out how much these benefits might be, call the Social Security Administration at (800) 937-2000 and ask for one copy of Form SSA 7004 for each income earner in the family. Fill out the forms and return them. You'll receive an answer in around four weeks.

Subtract any Social Security survivor's benefits and job-related insurance benefits from your estimate of how much will be needed for life-style adjustment. Add that result to your estimates on funeral costs and debt payments. The total is how much life insurance you need. (Make sure both partners in a two-income household go through this process.)

If you have life insurance from your job, you can factor that in as well. Just make sure to check if the insurance is valid for as long as you live or only for as long as you work at that particular job. If the latter is the case, you'll need to increase your own coverage if you lose your current job.

You can use the worksheet on page 128 to calculate your life insurance needs and those of your spouse.

Types of Life Insurance Policies

There are two basic types of life insurance policies: term and whole life. Universal life and variable life policies are variations on whole life. Second-to-die life insurance is an estate-planning tool more than a protection from catastrophe, and that's why I'll be addressing it in chapter 7, when I talk about your parents.

Term insurance is pure insurance. It's in effect for a specified period of time (hence, the name *term*), typically one year, five years, or ten years. At the end of the term it must be renewed, invariably for a higher premium. In most cases, it's guaranteed renewable up to at least age sixty-five. Term pays a benefit only upon the death of the insured. It has no cash value. The premiums on term insurance policies accurately reflect risk: They start off low when you are young and unlikely to die and increase as you get older and the likelihood of death increases. A $100,000 term policy would cost a thirty-year-old about $160 a year, a forty-year-old about $190 a year, and a fifty-year-old about $320 a year.

Whole life insurance policies are in effect for as long as you live (hence, the name *whole life*). Insurance sellers love to call these policies "permanent" in an effort to promote them. Whole life policies combine an investment or savings element in with the insurance coverage, so the policy can be cashed in without the policyholder having to die. Whole life policies also have a cash value that can be borrowed against. The premiums on whole life polices do not correspond with the level or risk, since they are the same for your entire life. That means you'll be paying much more than you should in the early years and much less than you should when you're older. On average, your annual premium for a whole life policy will be seven times higher than your annual premium for a term policy with the same level of coverage.

Insurance sellers do everything possible to push whole life, since they make more money on it. Up to 80 percent of the money you pay in premiums during the first year of a whole life policy go directly to the seller. Unscrupulous sellers will tout it as an investment vehicle and display reams of computer printouts with astounding projected yields. More honest sellers will point out that the guaranteed yield is generally around 4 percent and will promote it as a form of enforced savings. All sellers will claim that term insurance will be too expensive for you when you're older.

What they won't point out is that your need for life insurance should actually decrease as you get older. That's because your debts should be decreasing and you'll have built up some personal wealth by then (based on the principles I'll be offering in chapter 9), allowing you to become more of a self-insurer. Therefore, term actually fits your needs very nicely. While the premiums may go up every five years, your insurance needs will drop every five years as well. By renewing for your now reduced needs, you should be able to keep your premiums fairly level. And you'll do better investing money on your own than letting an insurance company do it for you.

My advice is to calculate your needs carefully and then buy enough five-year, guaranteed-renewable term insurance to cover them.

Judging an Insurance Company's Health

It's essential to check the health of an insurance company before you buy one of its policies. Insurers are no longer the Rocks of Gibraltar of the financial industry. Many got into trouble with junk bonds and poor real estate investments in the 1980s. It's actually more important to check an insurer's health than it is to investigate a company you're considering investing in. You're counting on the insurer being solvent much further into the future than you're probably counting on the investment being sound. Don't trust an insurance seller's estimation of stability—do your own research. The four financial-analysis firms that rate insurance companies' health are A. M. Best, Standard & Poor's, Moody's, and Duff & Phelps. Ask the reference librarian at your local library for help in finding these ratings. Don't buy a policy from an insurer that receives anything less than a "good" rating from any analysis firm.

Shopping for Insurance

Never buy insurance from an agent. These sellers represent only one or two companies with noncompetitive product lines. Insurance brokers, on the other hand, can sell products from a variety of insurers. Look for a broker in your area who has been in business for more than five years and who is a certified life underwriter (CLU) and a certified insurance consultant (CIC). While neither of these credentials is a guarantee of ethics, they do demonstrate professional education. Present your broker with a list of your requirements and ask for three to five different options to choose from. If none of the choices satisfies you fully, find a second broker and ask for more options.

Shopping for Term Life Insurance Policies

Even though I'm advising you to buy the simplest life insurance product around, there are some things you should look out for.

- The best way to compare term policies is by their interest-adjusted net-cost index. This is a complicated calculation that results in a cost per $100 of coverage. All you need to know is that the lower the cost per $100 of coverage, the better the policy. By law the insurer must provide you with this number if you ask for it.
- Make sure the policies are guaranteed renewable for as long as you want, regardless of your health.
- Ask for a printout of at least five years' worth of premiums. Some policies lure you in with a very low first two years and then increase rates dramatically, figuring you'll be too lazy to switch. You want steady premiums for five years.
- Don't buy life insurance from mail-order companies, at airports, over the telephone, from baby-food companies, or in

response to a television ad; these are almost always rip-offs.

- Stay away from options that pay more if you die in a certain manner. Your survivors' needs are the same regardless of how you die.
- Similarly, avoid options that offer partial payment for certain injuries. Medical expenses should be covered by health insurance, and possible loss of income should be covered by disability insurance.
- There are telephone hot lines available that will provide you with insurance price quotes for a reasonable fee. The only one I know of that isn't affiliated with someone selling insurance is Insurance Information at (800) 472-5800. Be aware, however, that they'll be quoting "preferred rates" that apply to only the healthiest of candidates.
- If you live in New York, New Jersey, or Connecticut, consider purchasing savings bank life insurance. These policies are probably the cheapest good-quality term products around.
- Investigate whether a "living benefit option" is available. This offers partial payment of the policy prior to death, allowing the funds to be used for nursing-home or hospice care. While there are third parties that will provide a similar service, there's less chance of fraud if the original insurer provides the service.

Now that you've secured, streamlined, and insured your stream of income, you're ready to start addressing your actual, rather than assumed, responsibilities to your parents and children.

Chapter Seven

Helping Aging Parents Take Charge of Their Lives

If you're middle class it pays to be of sound mind . . . or to die
quickly. If your parent is middle class and gets cancer her
bills will be paid by health insurance or Medicare. But if she
has Alzheimer's or suffers a stroke she'll become impoverished
. . . one way or another.
    —Peter Strauss, elder law attorney with Fink Weinberger

The fifth step in surviving the squeeze is to help your parents
take charge of their lives. About 25 percent of the 35 million
people who are sixty-five years old or older will need to go into
a nursing home for at least a year. Calculations on the average
length of stay in a nursing home are somewhat tricky to make,
since the guidelines and regulations change nearly every year.
Conventional wisdom puts the figure at anywhere from thirty
to thirty-six months. Strictly convalescent stays in skilled nursing facilities will be shorter, while primarily custodial stays in
nonskilled facilities may last considerably longer. About 10 percent of those who enter nursing homes will stay in the home for
five years or more.

Multiply the typical stay by an average cost of around
$6,100 per month for a good home in a metropolitan area and
the bill adds up to anywhere from $180,000 to $220,000.
Home care is no bargain, either. Costs range from $90 to $120

per day. Based on the same duration of care, the tab could come to anywhere from $81,000 to $130,000. With numbers like these facing them, is it any wonder that this has become a nightmare scenario for many of my baby boomer clients?

As I explained in chapter 1, if you're like most baby boomers, it's simply impossible for you to pick up the cost of your parent's long-term care. In many cases, your parent will actually be able to pay for her own care; and even if she can't, government programs can be tapped.

But just because you don't have a financial responsibility to your parent doesn't mean you shouldn't play a role in the rest of her life. You can, and should, serve as a guide, counselor, and adviser, helping her help herself. And that doesn't just refer to nursing-home care. Because of the huge numbers batted around, many baby boomers have fixated on nursing homes, not realizing there's much more to dealing with an aging parent. Your involvement in your parent's life should be an ongoing process, not a sudden reaction to a crisis.

That's how I've approached this chapter. It's set up as a step-by-step tour through the entire process, from your initial involvement to your final responsibilities. Of necessity, it's a long chapter, but bear with me. Even if you have an immediate problem, try not to jump ahead to the section that addresses it specifically. It won't take that long to read through the whole chapter, and by having an understanding of the entire elder-care system, you'll be better prepared to do everything you can for your parent.

One other note before I begin: Throughout this chapter I'll be referring to your aging parent as being alone and female. That's because statistics show that the highest risk group is those who are living alone and comprises primarily women who have outlived their husbands. Despite the pronouns, all of the advice and information in the chapter applies equally to couples and men living alone.

There are three stages in the elder-care process, representing noticeable shifts in your parent's ability to be emotionally, financially, or physically independent.

The First Stage: An Opportunity for Planning

While theoretically the time to start planning should be as soon as a parent reaches age sixty, most families wait until there is some noticeable change in the parent's behavior or attitude. I encourage you not to wait that long, but I assume that many of you already have. This complacency usually ends when it becomes clear that your parent perceives she has diminished physical or financial capacities, whether or not she actually does.

This is quite often caused by a shift from an active to an inactive life-style, brought on by either retirement or the death of a spouse. Frightened by the sudden decrease in her stream of income, perhaps feeling purposeless without either a job or a spouse to care for, and generally depressed over the changes in her life, your parent may cut back on her life-style. She may stop going to the movies or eating out with friends. She may begin to act like a recluse, shunning the outside world. She may stop paying as much attention to her diet, grooming, or health.

The best way to overcome this despondency is to enlist some outside help in convincing your parent that she is physically and financially able to take charge of her life and to simultaneously lay the groundwork for future elder-care decisions.

A Physical Examination by a Geriatric Specialist

Begin by suggesting that your parent be examined by a physician who specializes in geriatrics. Explain that you're not trying to rush the aging process but that it's important to add this valued professional to your team as soon as possible. Point out that a geriatrician is simply a physician who specializes in diagnosing and treating the health problems of older people. Just as a pediatrician should be the primary medical caregiver for your young child, so should a geriatrician be the primary caregiver for your older parent.

As people age, they begin to accumulate nagging ailments

that are often treated by a variety of different doctors. Surprisingly often these physicians fail to ask what other medications or treatments a patient is taking or receiving. Drugs interact in many different ways. You'd be amazed at the number of times depression, or even apparent senility, is actually a temporary condition caused by improper medication.

The best source for names of local board-certified geriatricians is your local-area agency on aging. For their telephone number call the National Association of Area Agencies on Aging at (800) 243-4357. Once you obtain the telephone number, make sure to add it to your Rolodex—you're going to become a regular caller over the next few years.

Have a Joint Consultation with a Financial Adviser

After determining that your parent is physically healthy and still physically able to care for herself, you need to focus on her financial health. I suggest calling in a financial adviser.

I advise bringing a third party into this discussion—and many of those that follow—about your parents for three reasons: First, despite your own expertise, your parent will probably always view you as a child. Second, since you are probably a beneficiary of your parent's estate, she may suspect you have ulterior motives. And third, it frames the situation in mutual terms. You aren't lecturing your parent; you're sitting with her, and together you're listening to an outside expert's advice.

In all your conversations with your parent about her future, it's important to treat her like the adult she is. The last thing a parent wants is to be treated like a child by her own child. Rather than "telling" her what to do, you need to convey that you're glad she'll be around for a long time but that together the two of you need to take various legal and financial steps to ensure that she's able to maintain her independence. The devices and tactics outlined in this chapter should be presented as ways for her to take control, not to give up control to you or anyone else.

How do you find a good financial adviser? Financial planning is one of America's newest professions. As such, it is still formulating its codes of ethics and standards. At present, there are no specific qualifications required before you can call yourself a financial adviser. The initials CFP after a person's name indicate she has graduated from a training course and is entitled to call herself a certified financial planner, but that's all they indicate. They do not represent adherence to an accepted code of ethics and standards or membership in a professional organization with peer-review practices. Anyone can become a financial adviser, and many salespersons—for example, insurance agents and stockbrokers—are using the title to wrap their selling efforts in the garb of professional advice. Until the profession institutes an enforceable code of ethics and standards and begins to police itself, vigilance will be left up to the consumer.

Look for a financial adviser with either an accounting or legal background. This indicates she has a solid financial and educational background as well as an idea of professional ethics. If she is a CPA or a member of the bar association, she can be held liable for her actions.

Financial advisers earn their living in one of three ways: by charging an hourly fee for their services; by earning a commission on the sale of financial instruments; or by charging a fee equal to a percentage of the amount of money they either save you or obtain for you. Work only with an adviser who charges an hourly fee. Those who work by commissions and percentages are more interested in their own income than in tailoring a plan that suits your family's needs. Similarly, avoid financial advisers who work for one specific company or who specialize in one particular type of financial instrument. Their advice is automatically biased. Your parent can expect to pay anywhere from $75 to $150 per hour for the adviser's services.

At this point, look for an adviser who has experience working with older clients. In subsequent chapters I'll be directing you to advisers with experience in other areas. The adviser you use now may or may not be able to fill your need later, but don't let that factor enter into your selection. Contact the National Association of Personal Financial Advisors at (800) 366-

Are Your Parents Rich?

They may not think so, and even you may not think so, but the government might, and that can cause you some trouble. The Internal Revenue Service hits estates worth more than $600,000 with at least a 37 percent marginal tax rate. (You would pay estate taxes on that portion of the estate that's in excess of $600,000.) In figuring out the value of an estate, the IRS looks at the current value of all the assets accumulated over a lifetime, including primary residences, vacation homes, businesses, investments, personal property, insurance policies, and otherwise tax exempt retirement savings plans. There are three common ways to avoid being hit with a huge estate-tax bill: Encourage your parents to spend their money so they don't leave such a large estate; encourage your parents to make financial gifts while still alive; or take out a second-to-die life insurance policy that will cover the estate-tax liability. Premiums on these policies are much lower, since they don't pay a benefit until both individuals have died. It's essential that these policies be set up so that the benefits do not wind up back in the estate; otherwise, they'll be subject to estate taxes as well. A financial adviser or experienced insurance broker should be able to make the arrangements.

2732—it represents only advisers who charge by the hour—and ask for the names of local advisers with experience in planning for senior citizens.

Meet with each adviser who is recommended. Ask for and check references. Make sure each candidate has been certified by either the Institute of Certified Financial Planners or the College for Financial Planning. As I mentioned earlier, certification is no guarantee, but it's at least an indication of education.

Look around the candidate's office. Does the adviser appear professional? Does the adviser inspire confidence?

Encourage your parent to be as open and direct with the financial adviser as she would be with a doctor. While you have every right to be in on the consultation or at least to learn of the results, you shouldn't be the decision maker; that's your parent's role. Ask the adviser to analyze your parent's income and expenses with an eye toward maximizing the former, minimizing the latter, and making an assessment of her ability to pay for her own long-term care.

If your parent has assets of over $1 million, she'll clearly be able to pay for long-term care out of her own pocket as long as her money is well managed until then. If your parent has assets of under $100,000, Medicaid will kick in quickly to cover the costs of long-term care. Those who fall in between will need to either take out long-term-care insurance—if they can afford the additional $2,000–$5,000 annual drain on their streams of income—or make plans to eventually divest themselves of assets in order to qualify for Medicaid. You and your parent will do the actual selection of a policy or divestment of assets a bit later in the process, when you've had a chance to sit down with an elder-law attorney. For now, your primary concern is figuring out exactly which option is financially viable.

Help Your Parent Investigate Community-Based Senior Programs

Stress to your parent that while she may need to cut back on expenses in her later years, that doesn't mean giving up hobbies, friends, or a social life today. There are many community-based programs designed to provide inexpensive, often free, cultural, educational, and social activities for senior citizens. There are even programs that attempt to draw on the expertise of seniors and offer it as a resource to everyone from students to entrepreneurs. Whether they offer simple socializing or the opportunity to contribute, these programs can help reinvigorate the despondent. Once again, information on such programs is available from your area agency on aging.

Examine the Emotional Impact of Taking a Parent into Your Home

Regardless of your instincts or past family practices, don't jump at having your parent move in with your family. There's a lot more to it than simply selling your widowed parent's home and adding a dormer to your own. Creating a successful two- or three-generational household requires careful consideration of the financial, emotional, and interpersonal issues of everyone involved. The addition of an older family member can exacerbate existing familial problems or even create new conflicts—if the family doesn't sit down at the beginning and tackle the complexities inherent in the day-to-day functioning of this unique living arrangement.

Unfortunately, such an invitation is often extended because the child believes it's "expected." That's especially true for victims of "the deathbed promise," when an ill or dying parent elicits a promise from a child to care for a surviving spouse. As I've said repeatedly, in order to survive the squeeze you must free yourself from such expectations. You are under no responsibility to take your parent in regardless of whatever promises you may have made under duress. Consider those promises to have been necessary comforts to the dying rather than binding commitments.

Even if you're inclined to take your parent in, it's better to wait at least a year before making any major decisions, because people are still in the bereavement process. You want to make sure the person who's giving up a home is thinking rationally, not just agreeing out of fear that the invitation will never be extended again. You need that time as well to examine your own reasons for wanting your parent to move in: Are you doing it out of obligation, or are you acting out of choice? The circumstances of the move are as important as anything else. Try to wait until the crisis is dealt with so that everyone involved is thinking with their heads, not their hearts.

If after a year has passed you still feel you want your parent to move in with you, don't encourage her to sell her house immediately. Remember: There is absolutely no guarantee this arrangement is going to work out. Rather than burning all your bridges, try a three-month "trial" period. That way, if things don't work out, you can at least say you tried, and all can go their separate ways, with no hard feelings.

Obviously, there are certain instances when creating a three-generational household is best avoided: when there's a history of physical, chemical, sexual, or emotional abuse in the family; if you and your parent have never gotten along; or if your parent doesn't like your kids. Such problems are not going to go away if you all live together; if anything, they're likely to worsen.

Since the trial period may in fact be the prelude to a permanent change in the household, it's absolutely crucial that everyone in the family—including your children—have a clear sense of how things are going to be run and what role each will play. One way to facilitate this is to draw up a family contract, laying down the ground rules.

- Is the extended family going to spend every waking hour together?
- Will the family eat all meals together?
- Are there certain activities that are going to be engaged in separately?
- Can your kids go into your parent's apartment or room whenever they want, or are there going to be established times when they know not to?
- Is your parent going to pay rent, or will she contribute financially to the household in other ways?
- Is an exchange of services (child care for room and board) an option, or is it an integral element of the arrangement?
- Who's going to pay for any needed home renovations?
- What if you have a gripe with your parent, or vice versa? Or if your child has a gripe with your parent, or vice versa?

Will disputes be settled between the individuals involved, or will the whole family sit down to hash things out?

While drawing up a family contract may seem an extremely formal gesture, it's better to have it and not need it than to need it and not have it. Consider it an opportunity for all parties to lay their desires and feelings on the table. Even after the contract has been finished, your family needs to get together periodically to assess how thing are going and what, if anything, needs to changed.

Examine the Financial Impact of Taking a Parent into Your Home

Before you take on the responsibility of bringing a parent into your home, you need to assess whether you can afford it. There's no need to be a martyr or to sacrifice your ability to survive the squeeze for some unrealistic expectation of what you "should" do.

How much should your parent contribute financially to your household if she lives with you? One way is to look at what she previously had been paying in terms of her mortgage, utilities, taxes, and insurance. If the figure you arrive at is more than adequate to cover the additional expenses of having her in your home, then that might be as far as your discussion of finances needs to go for the time being. However, it's imperative that you and your parent agree to review this arrangement in three to six months so that you can see if it's still working for both parties.

Rather than taking the money in the form of rent, it's better if you can get your parent to make a contribution to expenses. Taking it as rent requires you to declare it as income and subsequently pay taxes on it. In addition, using part of your home as a rental can increase your property tax in some states. A contribution, on the other hand, is tax-free, provided it's under $10,000.

Have a Joint Consultation with an Elder-Law Attorney

Though your parent may be in robust health now, some deterioration—mental, physical, or both—is almost inevitable. It's therefore imperative that you sit down with your parent now, while she's still healthy, to discuss what provisions she should make in the event she's unable to take care of herself.

As you can imagine, this is easier said than done. Not only does such future planning mean coming face-to-face with mortality; it involves discussing a taboo subject: money. For that reason, you should have an attorney present when you talk to your parent. Not only will an expert attorney help guide your parent in making the best arrangements, but as I mentioned earlier, a third party makes the process more effective and less stressful. The elder-law attorney represents your parent, not you. Explaining that to your parent can be the key to facilitating the discussion that must take place if you want to avoid heartache further down the road.

The search for an elder-law attorney should start with local agencies, such as the state or local bar association and the area agency on aging. They will be able to provide you with local referrals. In addition, if you know any attorneys, ask them for a personal referral

Ask candidates:

- How long they've been in practice;
- how long they've been in this field;
- what percentage of their practice is devoted to elder law; and
- what their fees are.

If possible, look for an attorney who works in conjunction with a therapist or social worker. That's an indication the attorney believes in a holistic approach to caring for the elderly.

For a free copy of the pamphlet "Questions and Answers When Looking for an Elder Law Attorney," send a self-addressed, stamped envelope to the National Academy of Elder

Law Attorneys, Inc., 655 N. Alvernon Way, Suite 198, Tucson, AZ 85711.

Your consultation with an elder-law attorney should include discussions of your parent's will, arrangements for living wills and health-care proxies, and an examination of Medicaid trusts and long-term health-care insurance policies.

A living will describes your parent's wishes about when her life should and shouldn't be maintained by artificial means. A health-care proxy provides the person named—presumably you—with the power to exercise the wishes expressed in the living will.

If your parent can afford long-term-care insurance, now is the time for her to buy it. If she can't and will be relying on Medicaid instead, there's still some time before she has to begin divesting herself of assets.

Encourage the Purchase of Long-Term-Care Insurance . . . If Possible

I believe the best way to take care of the potential costs of long-term health care is through insurance. The best of these policies will pay for a myriad of services, including nursing-home care, home care, day care, respites for caregivers, and hospice care. Not only do such policies keep your parent from having to artificially impoverish herself; they provide a secondary level of protection.

While there are ways, which I'll discuss shortly, to use the government systems—Medicare and Medicaid—to finance long-term health care, you need to realize two things: First, the government is in trouble and will eventually need to change the system; and second, the system may change after your parent has already locked her assets up. If your parent can't afford the premiums on a policy, she'll have to take those risks. But if she can, I think she should take out an insurance policy instead.

(By the way, these are two excellent reasons why you should buy your own long-term-care coverage. If the Medicaid system is still around in 2025, when the majority of baby boomers will have reached sixty-five, it will soon be bankrupt by the discrepancy between the numbers of people making claims on it and the numbers of people still working who have to support it.)

A policy that has a twenty-day waiting period, covers 100 percent of home-care costs, and pays out up to $150 per day carries an annual premium of $1,693.10 for a sixty-year-old, $2,740.51 for a sixty-five-year-old, $4,379.33 for a seventy-year-old, and $7,585.26 for a seventy-five-year-old. (As an encouragement for you to take out your own policy as soon as possible, let me point out that the same coverage taken out by a fifty-year-old would start at $550 per year and would increase only as much as was allowed by state regulations.)

There are some ways to reduce premiums while maintaining adequate coverage. Copayment plans are available, requiring the insured to pay a specific amount, usually expressed in an increment of $10 or $20 each day. Obviously, the higher the copayment, the lower the premium. Similarly, the longer the waiting period for payments to begin, the lower the premium. Waiting periods are usually set in increments of twenty days. If benefits are limited to a specific length of time, the shorter the time period, the lower the premium will be.

In addition, you and your parent should check with your state's insurance department before selecting a level of coverage. Some states are experimenting with long-term-care partnerships in which the state will pay the difference between costs and coverage if the individual takes out some level of insurance. In effect, this lets the individual qualify for Medicaid without divesting assets.

When reviewing individual policies, carefully check these points:

- What levels of care—skilled, intermediate, custodial, and home—are covered?
- How much is paid for each, and how does this compare to local costs?
- How are claims "triggered"?

- Are there any eligibility requirements, such as prior hospitalization, prior skilled-nursing-home care, or prior institutional care?
- Is there a waiting period for benefits?
- Are total benefits limited either monetarily or for a set period of time?
- What is the annual premium?
- Does the premium increase with age?
- Is an inflation option available?
- Are premiums waived when the policyholder is drawing benefits for either nursing-home care or home care?
- Is there an option that will let your parent pay premiums for a set period of time, such as ten years, then stop but retain coverage?
- Are preexisting conditions covered?
- Is Alzheimer's disease specifically covered?
- Is the policy cancelable or guaranteed renewable?
- Is the insurer solvent and experienced in handling health insurance claims?

The Second Stage: Laying the Groundwork

The second stage in the elder-care process begins with an actual physical or psychological deterioration in your parent's condition. The deterioration need not be major. Perhaps it's just that she can no longer push the vacuum cleaner around her apartment or see well enough to drive safely. Maybe she can't keep track of when she's supposed to pay her bills or forgets to take her medication.

While far from an invitation to nursing-home admission, such physical and mental lapses should serve as a call to action. These are signs age is catching up with your parent and that she needs some help in managing the tasks of day-to-day living. In addition, it's time to begin preparing for the time when she will need even more care in case she's unable to function on her own.

Unfortunately, physical and mental deterioration are unavoidable aspects of growing older. And while not every older person will need constant care, the odds increase the longer your parent lives. Anywhere from 30 to 60 percent of those who are now between sixty and sixty-five will need some type of long-term health-care services. And the figures go up for each five-year demographic cohort. By the time your parent gets to seventy-five, you're talking about one-in-three odds that she will need long-term care; and by the time she reaches eighty-five, the odds are one in two. That's why at this stage you'll need to help your parent arrange for some temporary help as well as lay the groundwork for the time when she will need total care.

Help Your Parent Investigate Private Home-Care Services

There are four levels of private, in-home caregivers: registered nurses, who are trained to give medical attention as prescribed by a physician; physical, occupational, and speech therapists, who can render specialized medical attention as prescribed by a physician; home health aides, who can perform paraprofessional duties, such as dressing wounds, bathing, and rolling the patient over for a massage; and personal-care aides, who provide custodial care, such as assisting in personal hygiene, general cleaning, and meal preparation. The fees charged for these caregivers depend on what type of organization they are hired through.

Home-health agencies are certified by, and work within, the federal and state Medicare/Medicaid structures. Their fees are the highest (personal-care aide—$11—$13 per hour; home health aid—$18 per hour; registered nurses and therapists—$100 per visit) but they accept reimbursements from the state and federal programs.

Home-care agencies are licensed by the state but do not accept reimbursement from federal or state programs. They are paid either directly by the individual or through private insurance. Their fees are less than those of certified home health agencies but more than the third option: registries.

Home-health-care registries operate like employment agencies. For a fee they will refer consumers to a caregiver. Good registries will refer good people, but since they aren't licensed by the state, you must be careful. The fees for caregivers obtained through a registry are $8–$10 per hour or $90–$120 per day for a personal-care aid; $12–$16 per hour for a home health aid; and $22–$25 per hour for a registered nurse or therapist.

In a few states the Medicare program will pick up some of the cost of custodial care in the home for those over age sixty-five—as long as it is deemed medically necessary. Otherwise, the cost of these services will need to be paid either out of pocket or by private insurance benefits.

Help Your Parent Investigate Community-Based Home-Care Services

There may be free or low-cost home-care services in your parent's community. The major source for information on such programs is the local-area agency on aging. There are hundreds of senior citizen centers in most metropolitan areas, and even very small communities have at least one. While these centers offer social, cultural, recreational, and health-promotion programs, they also have access to a wide array of other local services: reduced transit fares for the elderly; community-organized transportation services for those unable to use mass transit; in-home services, such as shopping, housekeeping, minor repair, personal care, and escort assistance; home sharing; and home-delivered meals.

Consider Hiring a Care Manager

If you find it difficult to assist your parent in tapping into these private and public programs or live too far from them to be of any real day-to-day help, consider hiring a care manager. Care managers are social workers and/or psychotherapists specializing in aging; they charge anywhere from $90 to $175 per hour, or $1,000–$2,500 per project, to help develop and implement a comprehensive-care package. Many work in tandem with attorneys who practice elder law. In effect, they can serve as surrogate children, helping to arrange for care and tap into local services.

For information and free telephone referrals of care managers in a particular geographic area, call the National Association of Geriatric Care Managers at (602) 881-8008. The national association will refer only professionals who have at least the equivalent of a master's degree in a human service field (R.N., M.S.W., L.C.S.W.), are licensed to practice within their own state, have at least two years' experience in the field of gerontology, and are the principal owner of a care-management business.

Ask potential care managers:

- What are their fees and experience?
- Will they supervise in-home aides?
- Can they help tap into entitlement programs as well as local services?
- Do they provide, or can they arrange for, emergency response?
- Can they help navigate the local nursing-home system?

In my practice I've found that care managers can often solve the problem of a boomer client's not being able to visit an elderly parent often enough to check up on how she's doing. A substantial number of my clients have parents who have relocated to southern states, such as Florida, South Carolina, and Arizona. My clients can't get down there often enough to truly keep tabs on the service being provided their parents. I've found that a caring, skilled care manager, while not a replacement for a child, can help bridge the gap between visits.

Have Another Legal Consultation to Begin Asset Reallocation

If your parent is unable to afford long-term-care insurance, she will either have to pay out of her own pocket or look to the government for help.

For short-term convalescent care your parent can count on Medicare, the federal government's health insurance for those over sixty-five that is provided as part of Social Security benefits. Medicare covers hospitalization, physician care, and, to a limited extent, stays in a skilled nursing facility. Medicare completely covers the *first* twenty days of such a stay, less a yearly deductible of $100. Days 21–100 are partially covered. (Medigap, Medicare supplemental insurance, can pick up the difference.) After 100 days there is no further coverage. Medicare does not cover long-term custodial care.

For that, individuals will need to turn to Medicaid, a federal means-tested program for impoverished individuals. It will pay for custodial care. However, in order to qualify for Medicaid an individual must have little income and few assets.

The rules and regulations regarding Medicaid eligibility vary from state to state and are subject to change. For the purposes of this discussion I'll be using the most recent numbers for eligibility in New York. You and your parent should, of course, check the requirements in her own state. According to the most recent New York regulations, a single individual, over sixty-five, who resides in the community can have an income of no more than $520 per month in order to qualify for Medicaid. The same individual would be allowed to receive no more than a $50 per month personal-needs allowance if she resides in a nursing home. A further qualification: Regardless of where they live, individuals are allowed to have only $4,500 in financial resources (a $3,000 luxury fund and a $1,500 burial fund).

A couple residing in the community must receive no more than $737 per month in income and have total financial resources of no more than $7,300 (a $4,300 joint luxury fund and two $1,500 burial funds) to both qualify. If only one spouse seeks Medicaid, the other can retain no more than $1,662 of the community (jointly held) income each month and no more than $66,480 worth of the community resources.

Other than an insurance policy, the best method of financing long-term custodial nursing-home care is to employ some combination of private funding and government assistance. Nursing homes allegedly do not discriminate on the basis of whether or not a potential resident is already on Medicaid. However, as we'll see during stage three, someone who can pay the higher private rates—at least for a little while—stands a better chance of being able to get into a home of her choice. The recommended technique is for individuals to retain enough assets to "buy" their way into a good home as a private placement, but then, once inside, qualify for Medicaid as quickly as possible. Generally that means retaining enough assets to pay for six months of nursing-home care.

By taking action far enough ahead, older individuals can legally divest themselves of ownership of the rest of their assets. In order for a transfer of assets to successfully be outside the reach of Medicaid, it must take place more than thirty months prior to the application. Anything more recent is considered an attempt to avoid seizure and is disregarded. There are loopholes written into the Medicaid regulations that allow even more assets to be shielded. Your elder-law attorney will be able to help you and your parent use the system to your advantage.

For example, some assets—such as primary homes; annuities that don't let you touch the principal; household goods, such as furniture and dishes; one car; term life insurance polices with benefits of not more than $1,500; burial plots; and some Keogh plans—are not included in determining Medicaid eligibility. By converting assets that are counted into assets that aren't counted, it's possible to speed up eligibility while protecting assets. Some techniques include using cash to pay off home mortgages, making improvements to the property, or putting cash into an annuity that won't be counted.

Your elder-law attorney may also advise setting up an irrevocable trust that takes ownership of your parent's assets but provides her with an income. If a couple is involved, the trust can be set up so that income is paid to the healthy spouse if one enters a nursing home. Of course, this means your parent will lose control over her assets. If that troubles her, she can also set up a revocable trust that becomes an irrevocable trust when she enters a nursing home. Trusts can also be structured so that income is paid to you rather than your parent in order to get around the Medicaid limitations on income. Remember: These trusts must be set up at least thirty months prior to applying for Medicaid for the transfers of assets to be considered valid.

Another way of qualifying for Medicaid is for your parent to give assets away at least thirty months prior to applying. There's no time requirement for transfer of assets from one spouse to another, but only up to $60,000 can be protected this way. It's important to remember that there could be tax consequences to giving away money. Gift taxes are due on gifts of more than $10,000, and any gifts larger than this are subtracted from your parent's $600,000 estate tax credit. Any assets exceeding $600,000 that are transferred from one generation to another through an estate can be taxed at anywhere from 37 to 50 percent.

A gift of a home or stock can lead to capital-gains tax problems. When your parent gives you a home or stock as a gift, the price that was initially paid for it becomes the basis price for figuring out capital gains. That means that if your parent paid $20,000 for her home and you sell it for $200,000, you'll have a capital gain of $180,000. On the other hand, if the home was transferred to you on your parent's death, its market value upon your inheriting it becomes the basis price for figuring out capital gains. In other words, if that $20,000 home is worth $175,000 when you inherit it and you sell if for $200,000, you'll have a capital gain of only $25,000.

The concept of middle-class individuals using attorneys to manipulate a federal program designed for the impoverished in order to protect their assets has its detractors. But from a practical point of view there are few other options. I believe that an elder-law attorney advising a client about qualifying for Medicaid benefits is no different from a tax specialist explaining the income, gift, and estate-tax laws to a client. While it may have been designed for the poor, Medicaid has become the only source of protection for middle-class individuals who cannot afford long-term-care insurance. The president, Congress, and the federal bureaucracy are fully aware of that—the loopholes are there intentionally. If you hear criticism of such Medicaid planning, ask the critic whether she has an extra $36,000 a year in disposable income to pay for nursing-home care.

The Third Stage: A Call to Action

The third and final stage in the elder-care process, which often develops suddenly, is a dramatic physical and psychological deterioration in your parent's condition. The determination that your parent needs constant care is both medical and emotional and occurs when a physical or emotional handicap prevents her from safely conducting the routine tasks of daily living: being able to get from one place to another; being able to feed herself; being able to bathe herself. There are multiple reasons for nursing-home placement, but usually there's one new mental or physical disease that is the straw that breaks the camel's back.

The physical conditions that traditionally force older people into nursing homes include memory loss, urinary or fecal incontinence, Alzheimer's disease, and difficulties with the activities of daily living. Diminished faculties can make everyday activities dangerous even if physically possible. It isn't simply a matter of your parent being able to bathe; she has to be able to bathe safely. If she has two major sensory deficits—let's say both her eyesight and speech are bad—that could make bathing extremely dangerous.

If your parent requires constant care, there are two options: She can move into your home, where you'll provide care, or she can enter a nursing home.

Weighing the Options: Home Care Versus Nursing Home

The most crucial factor in deciding what to do about an ill parent is to deal with the issue rationally. Don't simply assume that your parent belongs in your home because that's the way it's always been in your family. Decisions like this should be based on your actual circumstances and resources, not on some expectation based on previous generations' circumstances and resources.

Even though nursing homes are often considered the last resort, that doesn't make them a terrible option. They can help both the resident and her family. Often the structured, intelligent, well-managed environment offered by a good nursing home can be of tremendous benefit to a resident's condition. Home care isn't always the best choice. Sometimes a nursing home will provide quality of care that extends and enriches a person's life beyond just simply sitting at home with a cat on her lap waiting to die.

Family situations and conditions must be factored into the decision as well. There isn't a right time or a wrong time for someone to enter a nursing home. It depends on the specific circumstances. One family's situation may allow an elderly patient in very poor condition to be cared for at home, while another's may require that a patient who is arguably in much better shape enter a nursing home.

It is important to realize that potential caregivers have a right to live their own lives. Just because your teenaged son could watch Grandma after school doesn't mean he should. Similarly, just because your mother cared for her mother at home doesn't mean you must.

Explaining Your Situation to Your Parent

Don't be surprised if any guilt feelings you may have are compounded by your parent. She may say: "I took care of my mother, now you should take care of me." She may say: "Papa died, and you promised him you would take care of me." While

155

at the time you may have had every intention of honoring that promise, now, twenty years later, circumstances have changed emotionally and financially, and you're not able to fulfill it. You should not feel honor-bound to keep a promise if it's at the expense of your own or your family's financial and emotional well-being.

You can avoid such disastrous situations by putting all your cards on the table. Speak honestly with your parent. If she's under the assumption that you're going to take her into your home and you have no intention of doing that—or simply don't want to do that for whatever reason—you must be honest, admit it to yourself, and say to her: "We love you very much, but for the following reasons we can't accommodate you in our house." Then list your reasons. However, conclude by saying something like "We will, however, visit you, do whatever we can to keep you in the community, if that's your wish, and help you make plans for your own future." You'll be surprised at how this type of discussion can alleviate guilt.

It's crucial to keep sight of the fact that placing your parent in a nursing home isn't an act of cruelty or familial disloyalty. It's simply a response to the fact that you can no longer provide the proper level of care for her in your home or that the proper level of care is not available in the community.

Taking an Ill Parent into Your Home

If you opt to take your parent into your home, you need to realize that it affects the whole family; it should be something your family feels it wants to do, not has to do. Be honest with yourself about the amount of time you'll be able to give to your parent as well as the degree to which your parent is ill. You need to look at the emotional costs as well as the dollar costs.

Just as it's necessary to draw up a family contract and negotiate individual expectations when a healthy parent becomes part of the household, you need to carefully examine the addition of a sick parent to the household. It's a big adjustment, and the transition from nuclear family to care-giving family will be that much smoother if all involved know precisely what's expected of them and are honest about what they can and can't handle.

Those who opt to take in an ill parent are bound to feel pressured. As a combination caregiver, parent, and member of the work force, you're unlikely to be able to devote as much attention as you'd like to all areas of your life. You'll need to learn how to say, "I'm doing the best that I can," and believe it. You'll also need to get help—whether that means arranging for respite care so you can relax for a few hours; asking a sibling to take the parent for the weekend; or checking into adult day care for the parent. If you try to do everything, you risk getting so burned out you won't be able to take care of anything or anyone, children and job included.

Not only do you need time away from taking care of an elderly parent; you deserve it, and so does your family. It's not uncommon for caregivers to ask their spouse or children to help with the physical care of the elderly parent or to watch her while he attends to something else. Don't assume that your spouse or child wants to help you out in these ways. Talk it over with them first and see how they feel about it.

There are also some national organizations that may be able to provide information and advice on home care: the Alzheimer's Disease Association, (800) 621-0379; Children of Aging Parents, (215) 945-9600; the National Association for Families Caring for Their Elders, (301) 593-1621; and the American Association for Marriage and Family Therapy, which will provide the names of therapists who specialize in intergenerational issues, (202) 881-8008.

I can't stress enough the impact that taking an ill parent into your home will have on your life. My wife and I invited her ailing mother into our eight-room apartment. We thought that our home was big enough that, with the help of aides and other family members, we'd be able to maintain our lives while improving my mother-in-law's quality of life. We soon realized that one can't do that. The presence of an ailing elderly person permeates every room in the house and every person who's involved. It is a major commitment and should not be entered into without a great deal of thought and discussion.

Obtain an Official Assessment of Your Parent's Condition

If nursing-home care is the option you and your parent choose, the first step is to get a medical assessment of her condition. In order to gain admission to a nursing home, a form, called a patient review instrument (PRI), must be completed by a certified health-care professional—generally, a nurse. If your parent is hospitalized, there will be a nurse on the hospital's staff who can fill out the form. If your parent is still at home, call the nearest senior citizen agency and get the names and telephone numbers of visiting nurses certified to prepare PRIs.

A completed PRI can help determine exactly what level of care your parent needs and whether any specialized treatments are required—invaluable information when it comes to selecting a nursing home.

Enlist Help in Navigating the System

While a completed PRI form serves as your parent's ticket to enter what amounts to the nursing-home lottery, it's a mistake to play solo. The Department of Social Services, hospitals, and nursing homes are not your allies in the quest to place your parent.

Don't rely on the Yellow Pages, family doctors, clergy, or even hospital social workers as sources for candidate nursing homes. While some people sing the praises of hospital social workers who helped in a nursing-home placement, the fact remains that these individuals are caught in a conflict of interest. On the one hand, they are licensed social workers, trained to place the needs of their client above all. On the other, they are employees of a hospital that wants to free up beds as quickly as possible. Rather than relying on their ability to stick to their principles, enlist the help of a care manager, if you haven't already. The care manager's only concerns are you and your parent.

A care manager can look at your parent's PRI and suggest which nursing homes in your immediate area are especially good at providing the specific services your parent may need. At a time when you are suffering from pangs of guilt and fears for your parent's health and are simultaneously under pressure to get your parent out of your home or out of a hospital, you're in no position to make a careful, painstaking study of every nursing home in the area. By using a care manager you can at least rest assured that the homes they suggest meet their resident-centered standards.

Choosing Candidate Nursing Homes

There are three types of nursing homes: skilled nursing facilities (SNFs); intermediate-care facilities (ICFs); and custodial-care facilities (CCFs). SNFs offer the most intensive—and expensive—care, delivered by registered and licensed practical nurses on the orders of an attending physician, to bedridden or wheelchair-bound residents who cannot care for themselves. ICFs offer less intensive—and less costly—care, delivered by registered and licensed practical nurses and rehabilitative therapists, to residents who are mobile but not capable of independent living. CCFs are nonmedical in nature, offering assistance to residents who, while capable of independent living, may require some help with personal chores. In the real world, nursing homes can generally be divided into two categories: combination SNF/ICFs, and CCFs. The SNF/ICF facilities offer varied levels of care on separate floors or in wards, while the CCFs offer only nonmedical care.

Nursing homes are further categorized by their type of ownership. Proprietary homes are run by an individual, partnership, or corporation for a profit. Voluntary homes are run by religious, fraternal, charitable, or community groups on a nonprofit basis. Public homes are run by branches of state or local governments, are funded through taxes or bond issues, and are notoriously underfunded and understaffed. While there are some exceptional proprietary homes, I recommend voluntary

159

homes, since any profits generated are funneled back into the home, not the proprietor's pocket.

After establishing which nursing homes meet normal standards, the next criterion should be their proximity to your home. Placing your parent in a nursing home near where you live is important for three reasons: She will be able to see family and friends more frequently; there will be less wear and tear on the family; and you will better be able to monitor the care she's receiving. If the staff knows you stop in frequently, they will keep on their toes.

Find a Home with an Available Bed

Unfortunately, few areas have central clearinghouses that list which nursing homes have vacancies. The only way to find out is to contact each home directly. Place a telephone call to each home suggested by your care manager and ask if they have any vacancies.

Exactly how nursing homes decide whom to admit is open to debate. "Tipping" or "donating" is illegal, but it does take place. What is clear about the admissions process is that nursing homes are most anxious to admit residents who can pay their own way. That's why I encourage you and your parent to set aside enough funds to pay for six months of care.

Voluntary, or nonprofit, homes generally try their best to be nondiscriminatory: If a bed was previously occupied by a Medicaid-eligible resident, they will try to fill it with a Medicaid-eligible resident in an effort to keep the proportions of Medicaid-eligible and private-placement residents constant. On the other hand, they do have to bring some money in and are always anxious to find private placements. Proprietary, or for-profit, homes are under no such compunction: They have a certain number of beds they must set aside for accepting Medicaid-eligible residents and will do everything they can to keep within that number. What this all adds up to is that individuals who can pay their way are more likely to find a bed than those who cannot. However, being able to foot the bill for a little while is still no guarantee of finding a bed in the place you and your parents would like.

Dealing with Waiting Lists and Time Pressures

If your parent is already Medicaid-eligible or you're unlucky, you may not find any open beds, and your parent may find herself on waiting lists that stretch, on average, three months. During that three-month period you almost certainly will have to bring your parent into your home and bridge the gap in care with in-home aides, community services, and your own attention and care.

If your parent is hospitalized, you will be pressured by the staff to place her as quickly as possible. The hospital is within its legal rights to place a Medicaid patient in any available nursing home within a fifty-mile radius. You can fight such a placement, however, by contesting the transfer order with the assistance of your elder-law attorney. Under discharge planning laws, the movement of a patient from one medical facility, such as a hospital, to another, such as a nursing home, requires a written discharge plan. The patient or the patient's representative has a right to see a copy of the plan and disagree with it. In other words, your attorney can block the hospital's efforts and gain some added time.

Study Federal and State Inspection Reports

If you and your parent have enough money for her to enter a home as a private placement and you're lucky, you may have a couple of choices. Ask your care manager for further information on the homes that have vacancies, including copies of federal and state inspection reports.

Inspectors for the U.S. Department of Health and Human Services have a checklist of over five hundred separate requirements for nursing homes to measure up to. Every other year they visit each nursing home in America and note whether the facility in question has met or failed to meet minimum standards. While these reports have rightfully been criticized as being too cumbersome and too anecdotal, they can serve as a broad-brush portrait of a facility. Don't place too strong an emphasis on failures to meet standards not directly concerned with resident care, however—it could be indicative only of a bad day or a nervous aide. But if you find failures to meet important resident-care criteria—such as improper medical treatment or unwarranted use of physical restraints—take it as a warning sign of serious problems at the facility.

Visit Candidate Nursing Homes

If at this point you still have a choice of facilities, consider yourself blessed—you and your parent are among the few who will actually get to "select" a nursing home. Unfortunately, most individuals are faced with grabbing the first empty bed they can find and worrying about conditions only after a parent is admitted.

Never place your parent in a home sight unseen. Visit and investigate every potential nursing home regardless of how glowing the reports on it. If possible, bring your parent with you on visits; she will probably have fears, misconceptions, and qualms that need to be addressed by the home's staff.

Begin observing as soon as you enter the building. Is there anyone in the lobby? If so, what are they doing, and how are they acting? Are licenses posted or available for inspection? Is a "Resident Bill of Rights" posted in a highly visible area or at all? Do you notice any odors? A certain amount of odor is to be expected in the living areas, but if it wafts into the lobby, there's a problem.

During your discussions with the admissions counselor or administrator, ask what hospital the home is affiliated with. Get a list of scheduled activities for the week. Ask for a menu. Arrange to meet with the home's director of social services and head of nursing. It's your right to do so, and if you are discouraged from such interviews, something is wrong. Discuss costs frankly. Find out exactly what is included in the standard monthly fee and what isn't. Make sure your parent asks about everything that is on her mind. Finally, request a guided tour of the facility. If your parent has a specific problem—a broken hip, for example—pay close attention to the care—in this case physical therapy—she would be given for it.

Look around carefully. Certainly you should pay attention to the physical layout and appearance of the home, but also try to develop a subjective sense of what it's like to live in the facility. See what the rooms are like. Interact with some of the residents and get a feel for how happy they are. Remember that nobody wants to be in a nursing home, so everyone there starts off with a negative bias. Still, this should be the best place they don't want to be. Watch the way the staff speaks to the residents. Look at their gestures and listen to their tone of voice. See how the residents are dressed. All of these things give you an indication of whether or not the residents are treated with respect, are recognized as being individuals, and are asked what they want to do, not just told to do something.

If after seeing a couple of homes you're still undecided, discuss the pros and cons of each with your parent. Weigh her feelings heavily. After all, this is probably going to be her home for the rest of her life. If your parent refuses to acknowledge the situation or make a choice, it's okay for you to tell her that her refusal to choose gives you the right to make the choice for her.

In the final analysis, you really have to go with your instincts. You're probably going to be under tremendous time pressure and in a highly emotional state—there's no way you are going to be able to walk in with a ten-page checklist and objectively make judgments. Go with your gut reactions and try to confirm those feelings on later visits.

Negotiate the Admissions Agreement

Once you have reached a decision, there's one more potential obstacle to overcome: the admissions agreement.

Nursing homes require both the resident and a "sponsor" to sign an admissions agreement, detailing the rights and responsibilities of all parties and all costs and charges. Read this agreement very carefully.

Some nursing homes will also ask the sponsor to sign—either as part of the overall agreement or as a separate form—a financial-responsibility agreement that states that if for any reason the resident runs out of funds and is refused Medicaid, the sponsor will pay all costs. *Do not sign this agreement.* A nursing home cannot refuse treatment or care to a resident because of her financial status. If the home refuses to admit your parent because you refuse to sign the financial-responsibility agreement, stick to your guns or sign the document but write under your signature that you're signing "subject to your attorney's approval as to legal content." The nursing home can't require third-party financial guarantees but will try to force you into what amounts to an open-ended contract to pay thousands of dollars each month.

Keep in Touch with Your Elder-Law Attorney and Care Manager

Don't throw away the telephone numbers of your elder-law attorney and care manager once you successfully place your parent in a nursing home. Should you or your parent have any further problems with either the home specifically or the health-care system in general, they can help you cut through the red tape. They should remain on your team as an advocate for as long as you or your parent needs them.

One Final Responsibility

The final responsibility you have to a parent is to arrange a funeral if this wasn't done in advance. This isn't a "last gift" for the deceased. It's a financial, as well as emotional, obligation. Unless there are explicit instructions or plans in place, you should look upon yourself as a representative of the estate, not of the deceased. Your obligation is to spend as prudently as possible in order to save funds while still providing a dignified disposition for the remains. Love and respect are demonstrated by how much is felt, not how much is spent. The deceased is not concerned with the arrangements and will never express disappointment in them.

Prepare a list of exactly what services and products you need to purchase for the type of funeral desired. Remember that simple and traditional are always the most dignified choices. Carefully consider whether or not the item is really necessary and what alternatives are available. For example:

- Caskets are not required for cremations. It's perfectly acceptable to use an alternative container.
- If the body is to be on public view prior to the cremation, it's possible to rent a casket for this purpose.
- Embalming is rarely required by law and has no long-term effects on the condition of the body.
- Caskets, no matter how solid or airtight, do not keep a body from decomposing.
- Grave liners or vaults are not always required—it depends on the cemetery—and do nothing to prevent decomposition.
- Decisions on headstones and grave markers can be deferred until months after the death.

With your list in hand, telephone at least three funeral homes in the area and ask for a bottom-line price, including only the necessary and requested goods and services. Federal regulations require funeral directors to provide prices over the telephone. Don't visit any funeral home until you've made your selection. This relieves a great deal of sales pressure.

An excellent alternative to the traditional funeral that should be considered is to arrange for the immediate disposition of the body and hold a memorial service later. Most of the extraordinary costs of funerals center on preservation and presentation of the body for a public viewing—embalming, casket, and so forth. By arranging for either an immediate burial (no, or minimal, graveside service) or a direct cremation (no preliminary service), these costs are eliminated. A memorial service can be a wonderful conduit for expressing profound feelings for the deceased. Without the body present, thoughts center on the life of the individual, not her death. In addition, a memorial service can be held anywhere—perhaps in a place that held special meaning for the deceased; the choice is not limited to funeral homes or houses of worship.

Chapter Eight

Helping Children Take Charge of Their Financial Lives

It took the baby boom generation to turn the word parent into a verb.

—*Ross Goldstein, author of* Fortysomething

The sixth step in surviving the squeeze is to help your children take charge of their financial lives. To the extent you're able to instill in your child a sense of financial responsibility and a rational, rather than myopic, view of money, you'll have eliminated one of the financial pressures that makes up the big squeeze.

The relationship between your child and your money is a mirror image of that which exists between your parent and your money. While you're likely to become involved in your parent's financial life only during the last years of her life, you'll probably be involved in your child's financial life during his early years. And while you'll be working with your parent to plan for a time when she may not be able to take charge of her affairs, you'll be working with your child preparing him to become independent and in control of his own financial life.

Your involvement in your child's financial development should be an ongoing process, and that's how I've approached this chapter. It's set up as a step-by-step tour through the entire process, from your initial decision to have a child through your "final responsibilities" of perhaps taking him back into the nest after college. Like the previous chapter on parents, this one is also long. Once again, I suggest that even if you have an immediate problem, you don't jump ahead to the section of this chapter that addresses it specifically. It won't take you long to read through the entire program, and that will leave you better prepared to do everything you can for your child.

In the previous chapter I referred to your aging parent as being female. In this chapter I'll be using singular male pronouns when referring to your child. Of course, all the advice applies equally well to daughters and to families with more than one child.

The Decision to Become a Parent

I don't believe you have a responsibility to pay your child's tuition bills for him, but I do think you have a responsibility to provide for his needs until he's an adult and give him all the tools and information he'll need to handle his own financial life, including arranging for financial aid and student loans, if necessary. That makes being a parent probably the greatest emotional, physical, psychological, and financial obligation an individual can assume. It's something that shouldn't be entered into without a great deal of thought.

While there are innate biological motivations underlying the desire to have a child as well as a tremendous amount of familial and societal pressure to reproduce, I urge those of you who haven't yet had a child to make parenthood a proactive choice rather than a reactive or reflexive action.

Throughout history a great deal has been written and said about the profound joys of having children. As the father of four, and now the grandfather of five, I can attest to the rewards of parenthood. But I can also attest to the extent of the financial commitment of parenthood. The costs of child rearing are seldom discussed by people contemplating parenthood, perhaps because they think such conversations are crass. I couldn't disagree more. Just as you and your mate should discuss the emo-

Adoption Options

Adoption is a fact of life for many baby boomers, since around 5 percent can't have their own children. Yet, as abortion and single parenthood become more acceptable, the number of babies available has decreased. There are three major ways to deal with this problem:

• Private adoptions are those in which a couple finds a birth mother on their own and, with the help of an attorney, makes the legal arrangements. The costs and speed of this route vary, depending on how much is spent on advertising. Other fees will run from $3,500 to $6,000. Remember: No contract you sign can prevent the birth mother from changing her mind.

• Adoption-agency fees vary, depending on whether the agency is not for profit or for profit, state-run or private. Some charge only a nominal fee, while others work on a sliding scale or base fees on the birth mother's medical expenses (which could run up to $15,000). Most agencies require parents to be under forty, infertile, and married for at least three years. It can take two years to get on a waiting list and then another three to get a child; however, you run fewer risks.

• Foreign adoptions are arranged through an agency or an individual, usually an attorney, with foreign connections. Costs range from $6,000 to as much as $20,000. It generally takes about a year to obtain a child. Because of the potential for rip-offs and red tape, it pays to work only with a skilled, experienced, well-respected agency or individual.

Traditionally, most adoptions are "closed." That means there is little or no contact between the adoptive family and the birth family. But since the early 1970s, when the number of adoptees and birth parents trying to get in touch with each other increased, there's been a movement toward "open" adoptions in which there is an acknowledged link between the two families. Today between 5 and 10 percent of adoptions are open. In most cases, the relationship consists of a brief exchange of letters and perhaps a onetime meeting. However, in some situations, an extended family group is formed. The debate over which is better is still raging.

tional, social, and psychological impact of becoming parents, so should you discuss the financial impact. I don't think you can place a price tag on a child. But you should go into parenthood fully informed of the financial ramifications of your actions.

How Much Will It Actually Cost to Raise a Child?

Clearly, having children raises your expenses from the time the child is born until he leaves the nest. A couple whose oldest child is under six years of age spends approximately 10 percent more than the child-free couple, while a couple whose oldest child is between six and seventeen years old spends 24 percent more.

How does this increase in expense translate into dollars? While the actual costs of raising an individual child vary depending on location, income, life-style, health, and a number of other factors, it's possible to come up with some good estimates. The most accurate figures were compiled by *American Demographics.*

In order to account somewhat for the varying factors influencing costs, the magazine's staff divided families into three income groups. Low-income families are defined as those earning under $29,000; middle-income families, as those earning between $29,900 and $48,299; and high-income families, as those earning above $48,300. To reflect the scope of the expenses, the magazine included the child's share of housing expenditures as well as increased spending on food, transportation, clothing, health care, day care, baby-sitting, and education. And in order to compensate for inflation, the cost estimates are in constant dollars that have been adjusted to assume an annual inflation rate of 6 percent.

Here's what *American Demographics* came up with:

ANNUAL COSTS

Age of Child	Low	Middle	High
Under 1	$4,330	$6,140	$8,770
1	4,590	6,510	9,300
2	4,870	6,900	9,850
3	5,510	7,790	11,030
4	5,850	8,260	11,690
5	6,200	8,750	12,390
6	6,550	9,220	12,950
7	6,950	9,770	13,730
8	7,360	10,360	14,550
9	7,570	10,690	15,120
10	8,020	11,340	16,030
11	8,500	12,020	16,990
12	10,360	14,190	19,680
13	10,980	15,040	20,860
14	11,640	15,940	22,110
15	13,160	17,950	24,610
16	13,950	19,030	26,090
17	14,780	20,170	27,650
Totals	$151,170	$210,070	$293,400

You can't simply multiply these numbers by the number of children in a family to come up with the cost of raising a brood, since some costs will decrease with the second and subsequent children. However, you can assume that the more children you have, the more you'll spend on raising children.

Parenthood is time-consuming. According to a study done at the University of Maryland, women with one or more children under age five devote, on average, seventeen hours each week to child care; men in the same situation devote, on average, five hours weekly. When the child gets older and enters school, obviously the time commitment is reduced. Women with one or more children aged five or older devote, on average, six hours weekly to child care; men devote, on average, two hours.

All I'm trying to point out with these numbers is the extent of the financial commitment that parenthood represents. As the old adage notes: "No one ever has enough money for a child." And as history clearly shows us, most people who make the financial commitment to parenthood survive financially and flourish emotionally. But that doesn't mean you should decide without thinking the situation through or that you should feel compelled to become a parent.

Choosing to Be Child-Free

I'm not advocating either having children or not having them. While there are tremendous financial ramifications to the choice, it remains a complex and personal decision. But just as it's important to point out the financial impact, which is often overlooked or ignored, it's my obligation to say a few words about being child-free. (I use the term child-free rather than childless, since the former implies a conscious choice, while the latter implies some kind of failing.)

Historically there have been two common demographic reactions to decreased economic circumstances: delayed childbearing and increased numbers of child-free adults. The baby boom generation is no exception. As I pointed out in chapter 1, the baby boom is reproducing much later in life than its parents. In addition, many baby boomers are choosing to remain child-free. Estimates are that around 17 percent of older female boomers—those born between 1946 and 1955—and between 14 and 17 percent of younger female boomers—those born between 1956 and 1965—are likely to remain child-free throughout their lives. Surveys indicate that most of these women are remaining child-free by choice rather than by chance.

This isn't an indication of baby boomer selfishness, as some claim. Nor can it be completely traced to the new, expanded opportunities for women in the job market. If anything, it's an indication of the wide disparity in economic circumstances between baby boomers and their parents. The parents of baby boomers were in the financial position of being able to have children early and often and support them on one salary. The decision to remain child-free is an entirely justifiable reaction to economic circumstances. The percentage of baby boomer women choosing to remain child-free directly parallels the percentage of World War II–generation women who chose to remain child-free.

The Child-Care Dilemma

If you opt to have a child, nothing will point out your reduced economic circumstances better than the child-care dilemma. As I've noted repeatedly throughout this book, most baby boomer families need two incomes in order to maintain their life-style and, in many cases, to avoid slipping into poverty. That has meant that boomers, unlike their parents, must arrange and pay for outside child care. And once having opted for parenthood and outside child care, most boomers are stuck, since in order to pay the additional expense, they certainly will need both incomes. (Despite the need, only about 11 percent of employers provide any type of child-care benefit.)

Once again, this is similar to the situation that confronted the World War II generation. At that time, day nurseries were an accepted part of society, since women were needed in the workplace. It was only in the 1950s that these became a luxury rather than a necessity—since women could then afford to stay home and care for children—and were renamed nursery schools.

Debating the pros and cons of child care for baby boomers' children is a moot argument: If you need two incomes and decide to become a parent, you must obtain child care. Since that's the case, let's look at the three primary choices: individual care, home-based care, and day-care centers.

Employer-Provided Child-Care Benefits

While there has been a 600 percent increase since 1982 in the number of companies that offer some form of child-care benefit, the total still represents only about 11 percent of all employers. That's surprising, since providing child-care benefits—whether in the form of a company day-care center, a voucher system, or simply a referral service—has a documented positive impact on a company's bottom line. It has been shown to reduce absenteeism and increase morale, resulting in greater productivity; reduce turnover, resulting in lower training costs; boost the public image of a company; and provide a strong recruitment advantage. In addition, tax breaks are available for many types of child-care programs. The insurance costs and regulatory requirements, which are often cited as reasons not to provide benefits, are actually quite reasonable. For instance, insurance costs only run about $50 per child annually. Some experts believe that the dearth of benefits is the result of an information gap. Few senior managers (who are mostly males from the previous generation) realize the tremendous need for child care among employees—both male and female—or the potentially dramatic positive effect providing such a benefit could have on the business. Find out if there's a widespread need for child care in your company. And if there is, consider bringing the issue to the attention of upper management.

Individual Care

Individual care refers to having a single adult watch for and care for your child in your own home while you and your mate are working. This person could be a relative, a nanny, a baby-sitter, or an au pair. The advantage of individual care is that your child receives undivided, constant attention in a safe environment. The disadvantages are the cost and questionable quality of that attention.

The preference, since it addresses both disadvantages, is for a relative to care for your child. However, that places a tremendous burden on the relative, one he may feel guilty about pointing out. In addition, with most families now spread across the country, it's probably not even possible for a relative to provide child care.

Baby-sitters, who stay in the home while you're at work, and nannies, who live full-time with your family, are generally the second choice. However, the cost is exorbitant. Salaries range from $200 to $400 per week. You'll also be liable for Social Security taxes equal to 7.65 percent of the caregiver's salary, federal unemployment insurance payments equal to .008 percent of the first $7,000 in pay, and state unemployment insurance payments equal to about 2.5 percent of the first $7,000 in pay. The total will come to anywhere from $12,000 to $24,000 per year in combined taxes and wages. Even with paying these salaries you're not guaranteed quality care, since nannies and baby-sitters aren't licensed and most agencies do only rudimentary background checks.

The high costs and lack of a quality guarantee have led many people to hire au pairs: young European women, generally between eighteen and twenty-five, who are allowed to remain in the United States for only a limited period of time, usually a year. The average fee for an au pair is $100 per week plus room and board. Taxes are often ignored, since most au pairs are working illegally. While the costs are lower, there's probably a greater chance of having a quality problem, since au pairs generally have far less experience than sitters or nannies and the job is more of a lark than a career. And even if everything works out well, they'll only be available for a limited period of time.

The key with any type of individual care is to have a clear understanding of the rights and responsibilities of both parties. Is the caregiver required to do housework or cooking as well as care for the child? Are paid sick days and vacation days included? Does the workweek allow for certain hours and days off? How often is the caregiver paid? The relationship among baby-sitter and parent and child is very delicate, with lots of room for guilt, anger, jealousy, and fear to develop. That means everything should be spelled out in advance— preferably, in writing—even if it's a relative who is providing the care.

Day-Care Centers

Professional day-care centers are the fastest growing segment of the child-care market. At last count there were about sixty thousand independent facilities in the country, half nonprofit, and half for profit. Costs range from $50 to $125 per week, and care ranges in quality from pitiful to professional. Some day-care centers, particularly those affiliated with public school districts, provide true "preschooling." Others, unfortunately, are little more than warehouses for children. There are often long waiting lists for entry into the better centers. In major cities it's not unusual for couples to sign up for a place in a good center as soon as they learn they're expecting.

The key to a good day-care center is the staff, not the management. Incredibly, day-care workers rank in the lowest 10 percent of all U.S. wage earners. Turnover at facilities is high, averaging around 36 percent a year. If you can find a day-care center where the staff is well trained, well paid, and experienced, you'll have found a good environment for your child. Don't let yourself be impressed by governmental licensing of a day-care center. It's more of a revenue-producing tool for the state than it is a guarantee of quality or safety.

better able to absorb later on. Similarly, don't push the idea of saving money just yet.

In determining how much of an allowance to pay, be realistic—prices have gone up since you were a kid. At the same time, remember that too much is worse than none at all, since the child won't have to make any choices. Try discussing it with your child; you may be surprised at how reasonable he is. Speak to other parents as well so that you know you're in the right range. After setting the amount, agree to review it every month for six months.

This is also a good time to begin explaining advertising to your child. Try to explain that commercials don't tell the whole truth and are trying to make him want something. Don't expect him to turn into a pint-size Ralph Nader overnight, however. This will be a long-term project.

Ages Eight to Eleven

As your child grows used to the concept of an allowance, increase it annually, again basing the amount on conversations with him and the parents of his friends and peers. Consider broadening what the allowance should pay for as the child grows older. Perhaps a portion of it can be earmarked for gifts for other family members. Maybe it can begin to cover some of the cost of entertainment. Maybe he can even take responsibility for buying one article of clothing each season.

Ages Twelve to Fourteen

With the coming of the teenage years your child should begin to be included in those family budget discussions that have a bearing on him. There's also nothing wrong with beginning to talk about long-term plans like college. You may want to shift from a weekly allowance to a monthly allowance, giving him even more responsibility for budgeting and planning. If he has problems with that, you can always shift back to a weekly payment or compromise with a bimonthly plan. Consider giving him a separate clothing allowance over which you and he have joint control. A young teen may also be able to assume control over his entertainment spending.

This is the period when the consumer bug is likely to bite hardest, so be prepared for requests for advances. There's nothing wrong with an advance as long as it is structured more like a loan than a gift. Set up a repayment plan and deduct a set amount from future monthly payments. Make the term of these "loans" short enough so that the end is in sight. If he's becoming increasingly sophisticated, you can even consider adding in a nominal interest payment just to teach him that credit isn't free. Make sure to stick with your agreement on repayment terms: He won't learn to budget if he knows he'll be bailed out by parental largess.

Now is also the time to investigate savings accounts. Shop around for sympathetic banks before you have your child put all his money into an account. Some banks will waive fees, minimum-transaction rules, and minimum-balance stipulations for accounts controlled by minors.

Consider offering your child a chance to earn more money for doing odd jobs around the house, like mowing the lawn or washing the car. Just make sure these jobs aren't part of his list of ordinary chores. A good rule of thumb is that you can feel free paying your child to do something if you were going to pay someone else to do it.

Ages Fifteen to Seventeen

At this stage you can begin having lengthy, in-depth talks about college. Encourage him to open a checking account with a cash-machine card and give him responsibility for paying some of his own bills, such as magazine subscriptions and gasoline for the car. Discuss possible part-time jobs and business opportunities with him.

Most studies have found that jobs requiring twenty hours per week or less are beneficial and don't interfere with schoolwork. A job will not only teach your child workplace skills but provide an excellent, precollege opportunity for learning about time management, setting priorities, punctuality, dependability, courtesy, and teamwork.

If there's an entrepreneurial spark in your child, now is the time to fan the flame. Encourage and help him plan a business. The best are small-scale service businesses—for example, baby-sitting, simple yard care, and delivery services—that require little start-up money, deal directly with consumers, and don't have many adult competitors.

When my children were young, the family spent much of the summer on Martha's Vineyard, a small island off the coast of Massachusetts. At that time the island was very isolated. There were so many college students looking for summer jobs on the island that my high-school-age kids didn't have much of a chance to land one. They overcame this obstacle by launching their own businesses.

My son and one of his friends, realizing there were many New Yorkers summering on the island and noticing there wasn't anywhere for them to buy their traditional Sunday morning breakfast of bagels and smoked salmon, put two and two together and started a business. Every Friday when I flew up from New York to join the family for the weekend, I'd bring with me a load of bagels and smoked salmon from New York. On Sunday mornings the boys would deliver breakfast to those

Making Arrangements for a Special Child

If your child is handicapped or disabled to the extent that he may not be able to be completely independent, it's your responsibility as a parent to do everything possible to ensure his future welfare. In addition to implementing all the other advice in this book that's applicable, there are added steps you must take. These come in three stages, based on your child's development and your own life cycle.

From the Child's Birth to Age Eighteen

• Your first priority should be to name a guardian who can fill a parental role for your child in case both you and your spouse die. While the odds of that happening are slim, it must be addressed nevertheless. Similarly, make sure both you and your spouse have adequate wills prepared.

• Speak with a genetics counselor and share whatever information you learn with other family members.

• Try to establish a social network of other parents with special children. Not only will a network of people with similar needs help you cope emotionally, but it's apt to provide a pool of resources and support from which you can draw.

• Make sure both you and your spouse are fully credited and covered by Social Security, since a special child is likely to have a greater need for benefits. In addition, try to determine what type of government support programs—such as Supplemental Security Income—will be available for your child when he turns eighteen or begins living independently.

• Ask relatives and friends not to bequeath assets to your child without informing you. That way you can take such moneys into account when making your own plans.

• Look into possible employer pension benefits for the child. All other things being equal, it makes sense for you and your spouse to select jobs that extend pension benefits to special children as well as surviving spouses.

• Do all you can to ensure that your child is and will be as independent as possible. Investigate any public or private schools or agencies that could be of assistance. And make sure to discuss living and work plans for when your child's schooling or training is completed.

From the Child's Eighteenth Birthday Until You Reach Your Mid-sixties

• At this stage in your life and the lives of your spouse and your child, you should investigate community support services that your child could draw upon when you're no longer available.

• Make sure to investigate government support-service systems, such as Medicaid, that could help your child be self-sufficient.

• Speak with an attorney experienced in estate planning for advice in arranging for disposition of your own assets. Investigate options such as community trusts— in which you transfer title of your home to an organization that guarantees to provide housing and lifelong care for your child—and corporate guardianships—in which your assets are converted into a trust that provides a regular source of income for your child. Make sure to include any other children in these discussions.

Once You've Passed Your Mid-sixties

• Use these years as an opportunity to reevaluate guardianship plans and financial arrangements made earlier.

• Consider shifting responsibilities for your child to the designated guardian or trustee prior to your death in order to ensure that there will be a smooth transition.

• Finally, implement whatever asset disposition plans you and your spouse made with your legal adviser.

who had placed orders during the week. My daughters, realizing there was little or no entertainment on the island, began showing movies at the local community center. They sold candy and charged admission. Two of the girls have since become business entrepreneurs, while my other daughter and son entered into entrepreneurial professional careers as an actor and writer, respectively. I'm convinced that their current success is at least partially attributable to their youthful entrepreneurial adventures.

If You Suspect Your Child of Stealing

If you suspect your child may be stealing—perhaps he suddenly owns something you know he couldn't afford to buy on his own—don't be shy. Ask him about it. If your fears are correct, express your disappointment but offer to help him make restitution, perhaps splitting the bill in half. However, make it clear that this is the last time you'll bail him out. If it happens again, he should bear responsibility. If the behavior continues, seek professional help.

If Your Child Is Already Money Myopic

If the advice in this book comes too late or, for whatever reason, you're unable to follow it and you find your child is exhibiting signs of money myopia, don't despair. You can turn things around. I must warn you, however, that it won't be quick or easy.

Hold a family conference and discuss your feelings. Don't be accusatory—your child will tune out everything you say. Instead, state your case rationally and listen to his responses. After each family member has had his say, lay out the new rules and standards. Make sure your behavior mirrors the behavior you're encouraging him to exhibit; otherwise, it's a lost cause. Try to find ways other than money to convey love, pride, anger, and support. If your child expresses anger over not being able to get his way, let him vent his frustration. If you give him a chance to blow off steam and respond rationally, saying, "We just can't afford it," the storm will eventually pass.

Consider having him draft a wish list of things he'd like to buy but that he and you can't afford. Use this list when birthdays and holidays roll around. Make sure he understands that he won't get everything on his list. And don't let him add unreasonable items to the list; that will only lead to disappointment down the road.

If your child seems obsessed with the price of things, try to explain that money doesn't always convey value by pointing out nonmonetary things that have special meaning to both of you. If he shows signs of being miserly, encourage him to set up a goal and save toward it. You can provide a positive example by setting up a family piggy bank that you say will be used for a particular treat. Once it's filled, buy the treat, and then start over again with a new goal.

Helping Your Child Make Education Decisions

While it's not your responsibility to pay for your child's college education, it is your responsibility, as a parent, to help him decide whether he should go to college, and if so, to which colleges he should apply.

Should He Go to College?

As I mentioned in chapter 1, college has never been right for everyone. And that's even more true today when costs are so high and when it's the industries and jobs that don't require college degrees—hospitality, construction, health care, technician positions—that are offering the most job opportunities. If your child isn't yet in high school, by the time he graduates there may be alternative, noncollegiate avenues for advanced education, such as corporate-sponsored apprenticeship programs and vocational schools.

The decision of whether or not to go to college is obviously unique for every child and family. It depends on personality, skills, intelligence, interests, motivations, and a host of other factors. The most I can do is stress the need for an open mind, suggest early and ongoing discussions between you and your child, and offer some general guidelines.

I believe college is a means to an end, while education is an end in itself. Your child doesn't need to go to college to get an education, whether it's in art history or computer programming. He should go to college to get a degree. And he should pursue a degree because he needs it in the career he's considering.

There are four basic career tracks in America: nontechnical, technical, creative, and professional. By determining which track your child would like to pursue, you can make at least a general judgment on whether he needs to go to college.

- Those on the nontechnical track do primarily physical labor, which may or may not require skills but which doesn't require the use of advanced information technology. They include carpenters and construction workers as well as health-care aides and housekeepers. If your child wants to pursue a career on the nontechnical track, he need not go to college. He should probably pursue some type of apprenticeship program instead.
- Those on the technical track specialize in using, developing, or repairing advanced technology. They include lab technicians and clerical workers as well as computer-system operators and electronic-equipment service people. If your child is interested in a career on the technical track, he probably doesn't need college, either—at least not the traditional four-year approach. He would be better off pursuing technical competency through training programs or vocational education.
- Those on the creative track specialize in using their own artistry. They include writers, chefs, entrepreneurs, artists, illustrators, designers, photographers, filmmakers, actors, and dancers. If your child is interested in one of the creative fields, he'll have to make some decisions. For these individuals a college education is a plus but not a necessity. It may

provide either an initial career boost or a safety net, but it won't, in the end, have any bearing on career success.

- The professional track consists of those people who are in one of the service professions—doctors, lawyers, dentists, nurses, bankers, accountants, architects, financial advisers, teachers, journalists—and those who are in the supervisory level of one of the three business disciplines—management, finance, or marketing. If your child wants to pursue a career on this track, he will almost certainly have to go to college.

Remember that the decision your child makes today about college isn't etched in stone. He can always change his mind. Just because most people go to college directly after high school doesn't mean your child can't go later on, after being in the workplace for a few years. In fact, he may be better off waiting and learning more about his interests and skills. Those who have some work experience prior to college often make the best students. They're generally more motivated and dedicated and tend to bring a more mature approach to the college experience. If your son has worked in the job market for two years prior to going to college, it's less likely he'll party late every night and then need to pull all-nighters prior to every exam.

(If your child is leaning away from college, I highly recommend that he, and you, take a look at Harlow G. Unger's book *But What If I Don't Want to Go to College?: A Guide to Successful Careers Through Alternative Education*, published by Facts On File in 1992.)

Making General Education Decisions

If your child decides he should pursue a college education, he needs to make some general decisions before he starts judging individual colleges. While some of these decisions have financial ramifications, at this point you and he shouldn't let money enter into the picture.

❖ *Stay at home versus go away.* Unless you live in a very rural part of the country, there are probably colleges and universities within commuting distance of your home. By attending a local college and living at home, your child will have the advantage of a protective, supportive environment. By going away to school, however, your child will have a chance to learn independent living skills. This is always a tough decision. You may not think your child is mature enough to move away from home, but if he doesn't move away, he may never develop that maturity. My advice is, when in doubt, children should leave the nest. After all, they can always return if they crash.

❖ *Two-year college versus four-year college.* Junior colleges that offer two-year associate degrees fill a very important niche in higher education. They are, among other things, an interim step between high school and college, offering students a way to ease into the more demanding college environment. If your child has been a diligent student throughout high school, he's probably ready for a four-year college environment. But if he hasn't shown the dedication necessary, a two-year college will give him a chance to acquire and hone good study skills. I'm a big fan of two-year colleges for this as well as other reasons I'll get into later when I discuss finances.

❖ *Small college versus large college.* This is another difficult decision. Generally, small colleges offer more individualized attention, while large schools have better facilities and a greater variety of activities and programs. This decision should be based on your child's personality. If he's an underachiever or needs to be prodded now and then, a small school is probably better for him. It will give him a chance to get more individualized attention and encouragement and won't provide him with opportunities to fade into the woodwork. If your child is an overachiever and is a self-starter, a large school may be better, since it will provide him with more opportunities and his personality will ensure that he won't get lost in the crowd.

❖ *Specialized college versus broad-based university.* Another choice your child will need to make early on is whether he wants to attend either a specialized college or one that offers a more broad based education. Specialized colleges are usually branches of major universities. They generally offer highly regimented courses of study designed to turn out experts in their particular field. However, they usually offer students little chance to explore other disciplines. Examples are engineering schools and architectural schools that have very strict requirements about what courses students must take and when they must take them. These specialized colleges are excellent for students who are 100 percent certain they want to acquire a particular expertise. If your child isn't absolutely positive he wants to be an engineer, he'll probably be better off attending a more generalized institution, say, an arts and sciences college. If he decides he wants to shift to a specialized school later on, he can always transfer.

Your child's decisions about these four general questions will narrow the field of potential colleges dramatically. The next step is to judge each individual school on his list.

Judging Individual Colleges

The key to judging individual colleges is for your child not to let himself be swayed by savvy promotion. Colleges, whether public or private, are in competition for students. They do everything possible to attract students, from hiring Nobel Prize–winning physicists and successful football coaches to creating the most picturesque campus imaginable. All of this, however, is packaging. Your child needs to be a savvy college shopper and look beyond the hype. That means doing more than just reading the college's own propaganda. He should speak to as many alumni as he can and read everything written about the colleges. (Both *U.S. News & World Report* and *Money* publish annual college guides. I strongly recommend reading

189

their unbiased findings.) His goal should be to collect unbiased, objective information. Here are some questions he should ask about every college on his list:

- How closely does the college's mission statement match your child's needs and wants? Obviously, the closer the match, the better.
- How are grades, test scores, and extracurricular achievements weighed in determining admission, and how does this match your child's academic profile? For instance, if your child doesn't do well on standardized tests but is very active in student government, he'll have a better chance of gaining admission to a school that weighs extracurricular activities more heavily than SAT scores.
- How does your child's academic profile compare with that of a typical student at the college? Your child will be more likely to succeed academically if he is in the top 25 percent of incoming freshman. (He'll also have a better chance of getting substantial financial aid.)
- How diverse is the student population? The more diverse the student population, the more closely it reflects the real world. And the more closely a college reflects the real world, the better it is at preparing its students.
- How selective are admissions? The higher the percentage of those applying for admission who are rejected, the more prestigious the degree. Of course, that also means the college environment is likely to be extremely competitive.
- Is there an orientation program for incoming freshmen? It's important that a college do everything possible to prepare freshmen academically and socially. Some simply throw freshmen into the pool and figure the good ones will learn how to swim.
- What percentage of freshmen actually graduate? Is there a proactive academic counseling program? And are students who may be in trouble identified and helped? The answer to the first question, called the retention rate, is a very im-

portant statistic. It indicates both student service and student satisfaction. The lower the retention rate the more students are dissatisfied and the more likely they aren't encouraged to succeed. Look for a school that consistently graduates a high percentage of its incoming freshmen. The answers to the second and third questions will verify the judgment made from examining the retention rate. You can bet that a school with a poor retention rate has a subpar counseling and advisement system and doesn't bother identifying kids in trouble.

- What are the college's core requirements in language, science, math, humanities, and other disciplines? Are there cultural, social, and political activities?

- Is the college known more for its research than teaching or vice versa? Is most of the actual teaching done by professors or teaching assistants? And do students have a role in evaluating faculty members? Some major universities hire and promote faculty based on their research skills rather than their ability to teach. The most illustrious science faculty in the world is of no use to a freshman struggling with physics whose professor doesn't help him and who is relying on an inexperienced masters degree candidate for instruction. A college that stresses teaching will ask students for their opinions.

- What is the average class size for freshman courses? Large freshman lecture classes—of up to a thousand—are common at some major universities. Any student who isn't a self-starter isn't going to do well in such a setting.

- How extensive are the college's library, laboratory, studio, and computer facilities? Obviously, the more up-to-date and extensive the facilities, the better. However, make sure the facilities are used for teaching and not just research.

- Finally, perhaps the most important set of questions: What is the cost of tuition and room and board? Does the college guarantee to meet a student's financial need? And is there a per-student limit on aid?

Helping Your Child Arrange College Financing

The traditional financial planning approach to paying for college tuition consists of four steps: First, assume parents should pay for as much of their child's college education as they can; second, project what the cost of that education will be; third, determine how much time the parents have to come up with the money; and fourth, outline how much money the parents should try to set aside and where it should be invested. It's assumed that only after parental resources are exhausted should the student turn to loans, aid, and part-time work. I believe such an approach is impossible for baby boomers.

In most cases your parents didn't pay for your college education; you did through financial aid and borrowing. Your parents may have supplemented your borrowing and financial aid with a stipend out of their stream of income, but in general they didn't reach into their savings for the bulk of your costs. Since you're probably in a much worse economic position than your parents were when you went to college, it makes even less sense for you to be expected to do what they couldn't. Looking at the numbers involved, the idea of your being able to set aside and invest enough money out of your already strapped stream of income to pay for most of your child's college tuition is almost laughable.

What Will College Cost Your Child?

According to the most recent projections from the College Board, here's what tuition, room, board, and fees for one year of college are likely to cost in the future:

School Year	Public College	Private College
1994–1995	$6,334	$16,908
1995–1996	6,714	17,923
1996–1997	7,117	18,998

School Year	Public College	Private College
1997–1998	7,544	20,138
1998–1999	7,996	21,347
1999–2000	8,476	22,627
2000–2001	8,985	23,985
2001–2002	9,524	25,424
2002–2003	10,095	26,950
2003–2004	10,701	28,567
2004–2005	11,343	30,281
2005–2006	12,023	32,097
2006–2007	12,745	34,023
2007–2008	13,510	36,065
2008–2009	14,320	38,228
2009–2010	15,179	40,522
2010–2011	16,090	42,953
2011–2012	17,056	45,531

Let me take you through the traditional approach for a moment just to show how out of touch it really is. Suppose your child is currently ten years old and will be starting college in the 2001–2002 school year. Based on the figures above, the cost for him to attend college for four years will be about $42,000 if he goes to a public college and around $112,000 if he goes to a private college. In order for you to pay for his fees at the public school, you'd need to start investing $2,200 each year between now and his junior year in college in a financial instrument that earns at least 6 percent interest per year. In order to pay his fees at a private school, you'd need to start investing $5,800 annually in the same investment.

Not only is it difficult for the average baby boomer to come anywhere near such sums, but the idea of setting this money aside doesn't take into account your own need for disability and long-term-care insurance. I'm comfortable assuming you can come up with the money for those two mandatory coverages by streamlining your expenses, as I discussed in chapter 5. But unless you're either unusually affluent or unusually frugal, I doubt you'll be able to squeeze any more from your stream of income.

That means your child will need to come up with the bulk of the money himself. Obviously, he isn't going to get this kind of money from saving up his allowance and delivering pizzas. He's going to need to rely on financial aid and student loans.

While it's not your responsibility to provide the money for your child to go to college, it is your responsibility to help your child learn, navigate, and master the confusing world of financial aid and student loans. Of course, you and your child need not take this burden on alone.

Hire a Financial Aid Adviser

The first step in helping your child obtain financing for college is to hire a financial adviser who specializes in this area. Just as it was in your parent's best interests to have an elder-law attorney and financial adviser on her team, it's in your child's best interest to have a knowledgeable financial-aid consultant on his side. That's because, as I'll explain, the financial-aid system is very similar to the Medicaid system.

Since your major concern at this point is financial aid and student loans, you need to find someone with experience in those areas. It's unlikely you'll find an adviser who specializes in just those areas. Though there are such superspecialists, they are few and far between. Instead, look for someone who has a documented track record of having worked on similar problems for similar clients.

If you have an attorney on your professional team, ask if he has any recommendations. Similarly, speak with your tax preparer. If you already have a financial adviser helping your parents, he should be one of your candidates but shouldn't automatically be selected. (For more information on financial advisers, see page 222.)

The Myth of Scholarships

The first thing a good financial adviser is apt to do is dispel all the illusions you have about paying for college. The biggest myth is that there are thousands of obscure, unclaimed scholarships around just waiting for savvy students with good grades to claim them and obtain a college education for next to nothing.

In fact, an entire industry has sprung up around this myth. There are computer data base services that claim to work at matching students with unclaimed scholarships. These scam artists are charging unsuspecting consumers substantial fees. The same information is available free of charge through the College Board at many libraries and high schools.

But even if the information costs you nothing, it still may not help. While there are many unclaimed scholarships, most are for very specific individuals. The most famous example is the scholarship for individuals with one blue eye and one brown eye. Yes, there are scholarships available from corporations, but most are for the children of employees of the corporation. Sure, some foundations offer scholarships, but they are generally for students at the doctoral or postdoctoral level, not for undergraduates. And most important, scholarships generally do not lower your child's college bills.

The Concepts of Family Contribution and Need

You read that correctly: A scholarship may not reduce your child's college bill. That's because of the unique way that colleges look at finances. In order to understand the colleges' approach you first need to grasp two concepts: family contribution and need.

Regardless of what you or I believe and despite all the evidence to the contrary, colleges and the federal government believe that paying for higher education is a family responsibility. Of course, believing this way makes it easier for them to justify outrageous tuition increases and inadequate loan programs, but that's another matter. Colleges and Congress have developed formulas that dictate what percentage of a child's assets and income and a parents' assets and income should be used to pay for a child's college education.

195

Of course, if your child is independent, only his income and assets will be considered in determining family contribution. However, the criteria for considering a child independent are very rigorous: He must be twenty-four years old, be an orphan or a ward of the court, be a veteran, have legal dependents other than a spouse, be married, be a professional student or graduate student, or be judged independent by a financial-aid officer. The last criterion requires providing documentation of unusual circumstances. Basically, unless your child truly is independent, he won't qualify.

Colleges and the government do, however, give you and your child one break: They exempt a certain amount of income (about $16,000 for a family of four with one child in college) and certain assets, lowering the base on which they make their percentage analysis. (If you have an adjusted gross income of under $50,000 and you file a 1040A or 1040EZ income tax return, your assets won't be counted at all.) The rules about exemptions vary. For example: Congress recently decided to make home and farm equity exempt assets, but most private colleges still think you should be prepared to mortgage your home or farm to pay for Junior to go to their institution.

After the colleges and the federal government make their calculations and come up with how much they think you and your child should be paying, based on your income and assets, they compare that number to the cost of whatever college your child is interested in attending. If the cost of the college is greater than the amount the college and the government thinks you and your child should be paying, you demonstrate what is called "need." If the cost of the college is equal to, or less than, what the college and government think you and your child should be spending, you don't have need. The importance of need is that it determines whether or not you qualify for financial aid and how much you can obtain.

Let's say the college looks at your income and assets and says that you should be contributing $6,000 per year to your child's college education and your child should be contributing $750 per year to his own education. If the college's costs are $10,000 per year, it decides your child has a need of $3,250 per year ($10,000 minus $6,750). The federal government, using different criteria, decides you can be expected to contribute only $5,000 per year and your child should be responsible for only $500. That means the government says your child has a need of $4,500 per year ($10,000 minus $5,500). Assuming your child is accepted for admission, the college would offer a financial-aid package, consisting of some combination of grants, loans, and work/study funds, totaling up to $3,250. (The earlier you apply for aid and the more the college wants your child, the more likely the school will offer aid meeting 100 percent of need. But there's no guarantee.) The federal government, on the other hand, would offer aid in the form of loan subsidies—reduced and deferred interest rates and delayed payments—up to $4,500.

The reason scholarships may not reduce your child's bill has to do with the way colleges and governments apply them. Rather than reducing your family contribution by the amount of the scholarship, the colleges reduce your need by that amount. In other words, they use the scholarship to save themselves money, not you.

Let's go back to the previous example. Your child wins a $500 scholarship from the Kiwanis Club. Rather than applying the $500 to your family contribution of $6,000, reducing it to $5,500, the college applies the scholarship to your need of $3,250, reducing it and their financial aid package to $2,750. The same process is true of the government when it comes to calculating loan subsidies.

There are some scholarships that *will* reduce your child's bill. These are called no-need awards, and the problem is that they are few and far between and very competitive. The federal government, the individual states, and many colleges offer such awards but reserve them for only the most outstanding students. For example: thirteen states offer federally funded Robert C. Byrd Honors Scholarships of $1,500 per year to at least ten students in each of their congressional districts.

However, even if your child isn't an honors student, there's still hope. That colleges and the government allow some assets and income to be exempted offers an opportunity for savvy financial manipulation that can increase your child's need and therefore his financial aid and loan subsidies.

Playing the Entitlement Game

The possible maneuvers are endless and ever changing as long as the rules and regulations keep being changed. The basic principle is to shift income and assets from categories that colleges and the government include in their estimate of family income and wealth to categories that colleges and the government do not include in their estimates. For example: You could take money out of a mutual fund—an asset that would be included in college and government estimates—and use it to pay down your mortgage, thereby increasing your home equity—an asset that isn't included in some estimates. By simply shifting your assets, you have increased your child's need. If you own a business, you could accomplish the same thing by reinvesting your salary in the company. The important thing to remember is that these devices shouldn't hurt you financially. Unfortunately, many of the possible maneuvers have dramatic tax implications. That's why I stress the need to get a good financial adviser involved. He will know the latest rules and should also be able to gauge the risk and impact of any asset or income manipulation.

There are many critics of this approach to college financing. They claim that financial-aid planning, like Medicaid planning, is an example of the middle class taking advantage of a program designed for the poor. That's true. And the critics are correct when they say that there's a two-tiered system developing in America. But the two tiers aren't the rich and the poor; they're the knowledgeable and the ignorant. Knowledge isn't necessarily limited to the rich or the middle class. Anyone can go into a library and learn about how financial aid works. And while not everyone can hire a financial adviser to help them take advantage of the system, they could conceivably do it on their own. I believe that as long as loopholes are written into regulations—whether it's the federal tax code, Medicaid legislation, or financial-aid rules—there's nothing morally or ethically wrong with taking advantage of them. It's just being savvy.

Covering the Gap

Since the entire financial-aid system is built around there being some amount of family contribution, it's unlikely your child will be able to obtain enough financial aid, subsidized loans, and no-need scholarships to cover 100 percent of the cost of attending a particular college. There will still be a gap between aid and cost despite the best efforts of your financial adviser. Unless you or your child has enough discretionary funds available to cover this gap, you and he will have to turn to nonsubsidized loans.

There are three major commercial educational lenders that make moneys available to the general public: the Educational Resource Institute (TERI); the New England Education Loan Marketing Corporation (Nellie Mae); and the Student Loan Marketing Association (Sallie Mae).

- TERI and Nellie Mae offer similar loans of up to $20,000 per year with terms of up to twenty years. Your child will be required to begin paying off the interest on the loan forty-five days after the college receives the money, though repayment of principal can be delayed for up to four years. There's a guarantee fee of 5 percent of the total amount, and interest rates run one or two points above prime.
- Sallie Mae offers a wide range of loans. One of the most popular is the extra credit loan, which lets the student borrow an amount equal to the cost of tuition, room, board, and fees at an interest rate 4.5 percent above that currently offered on ninety-one-day treasury bills.

In addition, recent regulation has made Stafford loans, which are part of the federal government's subsidized loan program, available to everyone, regardless of need. The catch is that while payments on nonsubsidized Stafford loans can be deferred until the child leaves school, interest still accrues. In addition, there's a combined insurance/origination fee of 6.5 percent of the loan amount. Under the program's current regulations, freshmen can borrow up to $2,625; sophomores, up to $3,500; and juniors, seniors, and fifth-year students, up to $5,500. The total of undergraduate loans cannot exceed $23,000.

Of course, even though it's not your responsibility, *you* could borrow the money to pay for your child's college bills either by taking out a second mortgage on your home or by taking advantage of a program like the Parents Loans to Undergraduate Students (PLUS). The amount and terms of such loans would depend on your creditworthiness.

However, there are problems with this approach: It will dramatically reduce your already strained stream of income; and if you have more than one child, it will force you to play favorites. After all, you have only so much credit and/or home equity to go around. My advice is to have your child take out his own loans and limit your contribution to his education to paying for the financial adviser and providing whatever kind of stipend you can afford in the form of an allowance.

Reducing Bills and Coming Up with More Money

There are some less traditional ways to pay for, or reduce, college bills. Here are some tips and suggestions:

❖ *Negotiate with financial-aid officers.* To the extent possible, ask the college to substitute grants and work/study programs for loans. While it may mean your child will have to work longer hours while at school, he'll have less of a debt when he graduates.

❖ *Pit one school against another.* If your child is a desirable student—because of his grades, special abilities, or minority status—and applies to two competing schools—let's say Harvard and Yale—one school's better financial-aid package can be used as leverage against the other's.

❖ *Take advanced placement (AP) courses in high school.* Every college credit your child earns while still in high school reduces his costs by the difference between the fee for taking the AP exam and the cost of the comparable course.

❖ *Accelerate learning.* By cramming four years of college into three your child will save a year's worth of room, board, and other non-classroom-related costs.

❖ *Create your own work/study program.* Many employers, including some fast-food restaurant chains, will pick up some or all of the costs of employees attending college. And most colleges have employment offices that offer students help in finding part-time jobs. United Parcel Service, for example, actively recruits students.

❖ *Shop for tuition breaks.* Some colleges offer special discounts to children of alumni or families who have more than one child enrolled at the same time. Others offer terms on tuition bills that, in effect, can be used as short-term loans.

❖ *Double up with siblings.* If you have two children close in age, they can increase their financial aid by a sizable amount by entering college at the same time. The percentage of assets and income that colleges and the government designate as family contribution is the same regardless of how many children are in college. Therefore, if you have two children in college at the same time, your assets and income contribution are split between them, qualifying each for more aid.

❖ *Go to a less expensive college and transfer after two years.* By attending a community college or public college and then transferring to an expensive private school for his junior and senior years, your child can pick up a prestigious degree for half or two-thirds of what it would have cost to attend the private school for four years.

❖ *Become a teacher.* Many states will pay off some portion of the student loans of those who teach in the state for four years. (Math, science, and foreign-language teachers are most in demand.) By volunteering to teach in a "targeted" district, the child can sometimes get the obligation reduced to two years.

❖ *Investigate co-op programs.* Some employers, particularly federal government agencies, have formed cooperative partnerships with colleges. Students alternate between a semester of school and a semester of full-time employment in a related field. Not only does this provide funds for college; it gives a student a chance to build up a powerful résumé and network prior to graduating.

❖ *Buy à la carte.* It may be possible for your child to rent a room off campus and pay less than he would for room and board. Similarly, some colleges let students pay tuition based on the cost of their individual degree. This could result in lower costs for some majors. For example, a degree in literature would cost less than a degree in chemistry because lab facilities wouldn't be used.

❖ *Buy off peak.* Some schools offer reduced rates for evening, summer, and between-semester classes. The more reduced-rate courses your child takes, the lower his tuition bill will be.

❖ *Join the Reserve Officer Training Corps (ROTC).* In exchange for agreeing to serve eight years on active duty in the military, eight years in the military reserves, or both, an ROTC student can receive grants for the full cost of tuition, room and board, books, lab fees, and perhaps even a small stipend. There's a great deal of competition for these spots, however. According to one recent study, there were 30,000 applicants for the 5,700 scholarships.

❖ *Join the National Guard.* A guardsman commits to six years' worth of weekends and summer weeks. In exchange for this commitment, however, your child could receive up to $9,000 in federal loan forgiveness, a monthly stipend of up to $140, and/or free or reduced tuition at some public colleges.

❖ *Enlist in the military prior to college.* If your child enlists in the U.S. Army and earmarks $1,200 of his annual pay toward college, after two years of active duty the army will pay $9,000 or more (depending on service specialty) toward college costs. If your child serves in the infantry, he could receive as much as $14,400 for college after only a two-year tour of duty. In addition, as a veteran, he will be considered independent in terms of financial aid. Of course, there are risks to military service.

Making the Choice

Costs must play a very large role in determining which college your child opts to attend. While he may be able to borrow enough money to pay for the education he wants, the benefits of a particular diploma must be weighed against the tremendous debt burden he's likely to have once he graduates. If they are his debts, in the final analysis it's his decision to make. Of course, you should help him make it to the extent you can. I'll just offer two words of advice.

I believe that selecting a college based to a large measure on how much it will cost is actually beneficial to your child's long-term growth. The sooner your child realizes that many of the choices he will make in life are limited by financial constraints, the sooner he'll develop a realistic, mature approach to money. That, after all, was the lesson you were trying to teach him when you first started giving him an allowance.

The college your child graduates from will, to some extent, dictate how good his first job out of college will be. In addition, being a graduate of a prestigious university could open doors for him for the rest of his life. However, in the final analysis, his success will be determined by his own skill, perseverance, and dedication. Graduating from Harvard may get his foot into more doors than if he graduated from State U., but he has to have what it takes to get through the door and on to the next level. I've even seen cases where not having gone to a prestigious school provides a child with that little bit extra motivation and drive that make him a success. There's no doubt that a prestigious degree gives you a leg up on life, but it's an awfully expensive boost; one I'm afraid few boomers and their children can afford.

Returning to the Nest

Regardless of how successful your child eventually becomes, it is almost a given today that he'll be returning to the nest after college. Just as your salary hasn't kept pace with the ever-increasing costs of maintaining your life-style, your child's income probably won't be high enough to pay for an independent life. He may be able to pay for his transportation, clothing, food, and entertainment, but it's doubtful he'll be able to afford an apartment of his own. And while you certainly can't afford to pay his rent, I do believe it's your responsibility to take him back into your nest.

That doesn't mean you should pay his bills for him. Sit down and have an honest conversation about the costs of feeding and sheltering him. Work out a budget with him, allocating enough of his income to meet the increased costs he's causing the household and the rest to his personal expenses. Assuming that his income increases annually and he keeps his expenses under control, he should soon be able to afford to pay his own rent.

Even after he's out on his own, don't dismantle the nest. You may not be able to provide financially for all of your child's needs and wants, but part of being a parent is keeping the door open for as long as you can.

Chapter Nine

Taking Charge of Your Own
Future

*Retirement is actually a meaningless term. A person may
never retire and maybe should never retire.*
—*Gary Ambrose, financial planner, Personal Capital
Management, Inc.*

The seventh and final step in surviving the squeeze is to take
charge of your own future. That doesn't mean planning for retirement. I believe that retirement should be a nonevent for the
baby boom generation.

The idea of retiring from the working world at age sixty-five
is a relatively new one. While it was actually first proposed
back in the nineteenth century by German statesman Otto von
Bismarck, it didn't come to this country until the late 1930s.
At that point, with the nation mired in depression and unemployment, FDR and his New Dealers came up with what they
thought was a great idea: By providing a government pension
to those age sixty-five and older who left their jobs, they'd open
up lots of slots for the unemployed. It succeeded, since most
Americans toiled at jobs they hated and looked forward to not
having to go to work. And since those who left their jobs were
expected to live at most only another ten years, they wouldn't
need that much money to live on.

Retirement and Previous Generations

The first generation to adopt this idea was the grandparents of baby boomers. Since their peak earning years were during the Great Depression and World War II, they didn't accumulate much wealth. When they turned sixty-five, they were forced to rely on whatever pensions they had from employment and Social Security. For many, that wasn't enough to keep them comfortable, and they had to turn to their children for help.

The next generation to buy into the idea of retirement at sixty-five was the parents of baby boomers. Seeing that their own parents had trouble making it on just pensions and Social Security, they tried to set aside retirement funds on their own. They were lucky in that their peak earning years were during two of the nation's greatest economic booms. But even with that luck, what really enabled most boomers' parents to retire into a comfortable life-style was real estate.

When it came time for them to sell their homes, they discovered that values had soared beyond even their wildest dreams. During the 1980s it wasn't unusual for a middle-class retiree to sell for $200,000 a home she had purchased for $20,000. It was this windfall that gave many baby boomer parents the resources to retire comfortably, maintaining their life-styles without having to work. As I discussed in chapter 1, the reason for this phenomenal rise in real estate values was the huge number of baby boomers looking to buy homes. Since there was a limited supply of homes but a huge demand, prices soared. In effect, your parents' generation was able to retire comfortably because you and your generation paid so much for your childhood homes.

Boomers and Retirement Don't Mix (and Don't Need To)

How does all this apply to you and your future? By looking at the reasons for retirement and the ways it has been financed in the past, you can soon see that retirement just doesn't apply to you—and it's no loss. Let me explain.

There's No Societal Need for You to Retire

Retirement was encouraged in the past as a way to open up jobs. Today the reverse is true. The generation following yours is much smaller and, by and large, less well educated. (That's not a criticism of them; it's because your generation is the most highly educated in history.) Already there's a massive movement among businesses to hire older workers to fill all those positions they can't fill with younger workers. That will become even more pronounced as your generation grows older.

Baby boomers will continue to be needed in the job market for as long as they're around. While that may not mean you'll stay at the top of the corporate ladder or that you'll be able to count on having one particular job for as long as you'd like, it will mean you'll be able to find a job for as long as you want to look for one. The older baby boomer fits the employee profile that companies of the future will be looking for; you will be the answer to all their needs. Downsized companies will be on the lookout for experienced, independent contractors or project workers who can fill a short-term niche without needing the promise of a career.

You Won't Have the Money for It, Anyway

Besides there being no societal need for you to retire, the odds of your being able to pay for the kind of retirement your parents will have, or are now enjoying, are very long. First, as I've noted repeatedly, your real income has stagnated for years, while your expenses have climbed. That has given you little chance to set aside much money for retirement.

Second, while your parents could count on converting their real estate into a retirement fund, you can't. When it came time for your parents to sell, demand was high and supply was low, thanks to the number of people looking to buy homes.

When it comes time for you to sell, the reverse will be true. There's a very small generation following yours. That means there will be a lot more houses, co-ops, and condos up for sale than there will be potential buyers. That translates into low prices. Your situation will be more like your grandparents' than your parents'. Unfortunately, your kids won't have the money to bail you out.

(The buyers' market for real estate has had a dramatic effect on many of my clients who own apartments in New York City. Prices have fallen so far from just a few short years ago that today the preoccupation among many sellers is what kind of deal they're going to work out with the holder of their first mortgage. At least one-third of my clients are unable to sell their homes for enough to pay off the balance of their mortgages, so they're forced to go back to the bank and negotiate terms to pay off the balance.)

And third, even if you've succeeded in putting some money away, or selling your home for a good price, it's unlikely it would be enough. Your parents are in danger of outliving even their substantial retirement assets due to increased longevity. Members of your generation, who have been concerned with nutrition and exercise for years, will probably live well past eighty-five, if not longer. That means that if you want to retire at age sixty-five and maintain your current life-style, you'd need enough money to replace your present income for twenty years or more. In other words, you'd have to earn enough in about forty years of working (twenty-five to sixty-five) to pay for about sixty years of living (twenty-five to eighty-five). Conventional wisdom now says that those who have pensions should accumulate three to six times their annual preretirement earnings, while those without pensions should accumulate four to eight times their peak yearly salary.

And Even If You Could, Why Would You Want To?

Even if you could pull off this financial maneuver, why would you want to? If you're like most boomers, you grew up watching your grandparents and parents work in jobs they hated. As a result, you made a conscious effort to find "meaningful" work. For your grandparents and parents, retirement was a reward for a life of toil at something they hated. For you it would be a twenty-year vacation from a job you probably like. If you like what you're doing, why stop doing it when you reach age sixty-five?

I'm amazed at how many people who were active and alert at age sixty-four suddenly become sedentary and seemingly senile after two years of retirement. After a while you find yourself sitting around the pool discussing your gallstones or going to the early-bird special at the local restaurant. Traditional retirement is often deadening and life shortening, not rewarding and life extending.

I'm sixty-four and have no intention of ever retiring. I believe that if you like what you're doing you should keep right on doing it for as long as you can. And if you don't like what you're doing, you should start doing something you do like.

A Path to a More Rewarding Life

While initially you may think the approach I'm suggesting requires you to give up something, actually it gives you an opportunity to gain something: a rewarding life. Those who establish retirement as their goal are making sacrifices today for a tomorrow that may never come. Even if you scrimp and save and invest for the day you turn sixty-five, there's no guarantee you'll ever reach that point. You could get hit by a bus on your way to make another deposit in your IRA. Sure, I'm exaggerating to make a point, but I think it's one worth making.

Live for today, not tomorrow. Today is cash; tomorrow is a promissory note. Work at something you enjoy and do what makes you happy now; don't put it off for the day you turn sixty-five. If that means scaling back your life-style after age sixty-five, so be it. Life shouldn't be a dress rehearsal for retirement.

Rather than trying to accumulate enough wealth to stop working at age sixty-five, just follow the guidelines in this book and do the best you can. By taking away that artificial goal of retirement, you can change life from being a means to an end to an end itself. And that, I believe, is a lot healthier and a much better example for your children.

Changing your approach to the future in this manner doesn't mean you won't need to plan for your later years; it just means the planning will be different and far less fearful.

A New Financial Goal

Let's say you go along with my suggestion and abandon the idea of retiring at age sixty-five while maintaining your current life-style. You'll still need to take some financial steps for your future, but they'll be a bit different.

The Need to Bolster a Shrinking Stream of Income

While I'm encouraging you to keep working for as long as you can and want, there will come a time when your stream of income shrinks anyway. That will happen for one of two reasons.

For one thing, at a certain point, your income may grow beyond your perceived contribution to your employer. Despite your seasoning and experience, an employer may decide she'd be better off hiring someone younger who won't command so high a salary. Most people aren't terminated for cause. They're let go either because their function is being eliminated (downsizing) or because they can be replaced by someone who will cost the company less money. Of course, you will still be able to find another job, as I explained earlier. However, it may not be for as much money.

And for another, a natural consequence of aging is a decrease in physical prowess and energy. You may be able to minimize this through diet and exercise, but it will happen nevertheless. That means you simply may not be able to put in those ten-hour days and six-day weeks. Your experience and improved decision-making capability may compensate for reduced energy to some degree, but eventually you'll find you can't put in the hours required to earn the same income.

So while you may no longer have to set aside and invest funds to pay for retirement, you will need to make provisions for the unavoidable decrease in your stream of income that comes either through pricing yourself out of a job, slowing down, or doing something different.

Having a Nonspecific Goal Means You'll Have More Choice

Rather than your goal being retirement, your new goal is to establish an income-supplement fund. This isn't just a matter of trading one onerous burden for another. The goal of retirement was very specific. It required you to have a certain amount of money—enough to pay for twenty years or more of your current living expenses—by a certain time: the day you turn sixty-five. That meant you had very few choices about either how much to invest or where to invest it.

Your new goal of having an income-supplement fund isn't as sharply defined as your former goal of having to save for your retirement. There's no magic number or target date for you to live up to. The lack of such specific goals is empowering. By removing these benchmarks you gain a great deal more freedom in deciding how much to invest and where to invest it. Decisions can be based on your feelings and attitudes rather than your age. Rather than saying to yourself, "I must set aside this much for my retirement," you can say, "I'm able to set aside this much for my future."

Where will this money come from? Your stream of income. By streamlining your life and reducing your expenses you should have generated a surplus. Part of that surplus must go toward ensuring your stream of income, but the rest can be dedicated to growing wealth.

No one can or should tell you how much of your stream of income you "must" dedicate toward your future or where you "have to" invest it. Obviously, the more you can set aside and the sooner you begin, the more of a cushion you'll have later in life. How much of your stream of income you decide to invest for the future and what, if anything, you give up today to come up with the money are your own decisions. Sure, it's harder to decide yourself than to have others tell you what to do. But it's also more empowering. By opting to abandon the artificial and outdated notion of retirement, you actually seize control of your financial future.

Whatever your decision about how much of your stream of income you'll be able to dedicate to your future, my suggestion is to put that number on a new line in your monthly budget and label it "income-supplement fund." The next thing to think about is where you're going to put this money.

Investing for Your Future

Your goal should be to make your income-supplement fund increase in value as much as possible. As I mentioned in chapter 1, simply putting this fund in a savings account, money market fund, or certificate of deposit will not get the job done. Those financial instruments will do little more than keep your money from shrinking in value, and they may not even do that. When inflation is 4 percent, and the interest on a certificate of deposit is 3 percent, your money is actually losing value. That means you'll need to move beyond savings into the world of investment and figure out where to invest your money. At first, it appears as though you have many options.

Precious Metals and Gems

The oldest investments in the world are precious metals and gems. For centuries people have been acquiring and hoarding gold and silver, diamonds and emeralds. In modern times, whenever there's economic uncertainty, sales of precious metals and gems increase. That's because people feel that when the

Legal Advice for Gays and Lesbians

I'd be remiss if I didn't directly address the needs of baby boomers who are homosexual. Single homosexuals, with or without children, should do exactly the same things as single heterosexuals. Sexual preference should have no bearing on financial planning, and since money has no prejudices, it doesn't. Sexual preference shouldn't have any bearing on legal planning, either, but unfortunately, since our government and legal system have prejudices, that's not the case. Since the law generally doesn't recognize homosexual marriages, gay and lesbian couples can't file joint tax returns, share health insurance plans, recover damages when a partner is injured, receive survivor's benefits, automatically inherit property, obtain residency status for a foreign-born partner, or make medical decisions for each other. Gay and lesbian couples should find an attorney experienced in dealing with their special needs and should have livings wills, health-care proxies, and wills drafted immediately. In addition, if the couple will be mingling or acquiring assets, partnership agreements that spell out exactly how assets are to be held and divided should be drawn up. I hate having to pass such advice on. Such legal maneuvering tends to reinforce the homophobic notion that gay and lesbian relationships are less durable than straight relationships. In addition, like prenuptial agreements, these partnership agreements tend to plant the seeds of disunion. The solution is for the law to accord the same rights to gay and lesbian marriages as to straight marriages.

economy is unstable they're best off investing in these, the world's most basic valuable substances. They are physical investments that are easily transportable, allowing their owners to carry them with them when they flee. Many an immigrant family can recall how Great-grandma sewed jewelry into the lining of her coat in order to hide some wealth and bring it with her to the New World.

But regardless of the economic climate and despite their portability, precious metals and gems are not sound investments. They simply don't increase in value enough for them to be worthwhile. Look back to the Persian Gulf War. Even with all the fears of a crisis in the oil supply and the potential economic disruption that could bring on, gold prices did not rise very much. Those jewels sewn into Great-grandma's coat may have enabled her to bring some wealth with her, but when it came time to sell them in the New World, she probably didn't get back what she had paid for them.

There's nothing wrong with buying precious metals and gems for your own pleasure and adornment, but they aren't wise investments on which to build your future.

Collectibles, Art, and Antiques

Collectibles, artwork, and antiques are no better than precious metals and gems at building personal wealth. They may be valuable to another collector, but your collection of baseball cards, Warhol lithographs, and Louis XIV chairs aren't investments. Buy and collect them for the pleasure they add to your life, not for any effect they may have on your personal wealth. If your grandchildren are able to sell them for a small fortune, that would be wonderful, but don't count on their doing anything for you financially.

Real Estate

Personal real estate won't cut it, either. Your parents may have been able to build a substantial net worth through their purchase of a home, but as I mentioned earlier, demographics were on their side. You aren't so lucky.

I believe owning your own home adds immeasurably to your quality of life. It's also one of the few tax shelters left for the average American. I'm also in favor of owning vacation or weekend homes as long as they don't place too much strain on your stream of income. Having a second home can be an enriching experience for a couple or a family, making summers or even weekends memorable events.

Yet I must tell you flat out, while I'm convinced the value of well-selected real estate will keep pace with inflation, your personal real estate will not generate wealth for you. Similarly, stay away from investments in commercial real estate and products like real estate investment trusts. The commercial real estate market may become a sound investment again, but I don't think that's going to happen in your lifetime.

Bonds

A bond is a loan to a corporation, government, or government agency. The entity issuing the bond promises to repay bondholders their initial investment, plus a specified amount of interest, on a specified date. Bonds typically offer a much better return than traditional debt instruments, such as savings accounts, money market funds, and certificates of deposit.

Their safety and yield depend on the stability of the entity issuing them and the length of time before they come due. The more stable the entity issuing them and the shorter their term, the safer they are but the less they are likely to yield. Companies, as we all know, can go bankrupt. Municipalities, states, and government agencies can also have financial difficulties, while few will actually ever go belly up. The federal government, despite all the talk of massive deficits and debt, will never go bankrupt. Therefore, long-term bonds issued by a company have the highest yield but the greatest risk, while short-term bonds issued by the federal government have the greatest safety but the lowest yield.

Bonds may well have a place in your investment portfolio, but only to the extent that they minimize the risk of what I believe is the best investment you can make for your future: stocks.

Stocks

A stock is a share of ownership in a corporation. When you purchase a stock, you are assuming all the potential risks and rewards that attend being an owner of a business. When the company does well, more people want to become owners, and the value of a share of stock increases. When the company generates a large profit and wishes to disburse it, you share in the income by receiving a payment that's called a dividend. But when the company does poorly, the value of that share of stock decreases.

Historically, investing in stocks has been the single best way to generate personal wealth. The stock market as a whole has grown at a rate of between four and five points better than bank deposits or U.S. government treasury bills. There's no other type of investment that can make that claim. Let's look at the numbers.

According to numbers compiled by *Consumer Reports*, if from 1988 through 1992 you had placed $2,000 a year (for a total of $10,000) in the following investments, here's what you would have ended up with:

- U.S. Savings Bonds—$11,545, for an average annual yield of 3.09 percent.
- Bank certificates of deposit—$12,183, for an average annual yield of 4.37 percent.
- Money market funds—$12,368, for an average annual yield of 4.74 percent.
- Corporate bonds—$14,090, for an average annual yield of 8.18 percent.
- Stocks—$15,440, for an average annual yield of 10.88 per cent.

However, it's essential that you realize that this historic high yield on stock investments works out only when you look at the market over a long period of time. In the short term the market and the individual stocks within it rise and fall in value, apparently without any rhyme or reason. While there are plenty of investment advisers around who will claim they've figured out when the market will go up or down, they're selling get-rich-quick dreams, not sound investment advice.

I tell my clients that in order to grow sufficient wealth they should invest their income-supplement fund (and any pension moneys they have control over) primarily in the stock market. I realize this carries some risk, but I believe it's the best way for you to survive the squeeze and generate enough money to offset the natural shrinking of your stream of income that comes with growing older.

Minimizing Risk

Having said that, I must add that it's important for you to minimize the risk of investing in the stock market. The first way to minimize your risk is to invest some of your money in bonds. This approach is called balancing a portfolio. By investing in both stocks and bonds at the same time, you can ensure that your income-supplement fund isn't entirely subject to the vagaries of the stock market.

But there's a price to be paid for this. According to *Consumer Reports*, if you had invested $2,000 every year since 1972 in treasury bills, you'd now have $170,000. If you had invested the same $2,000 in stocks instead, you'd have $310,000. Even if you had bought those stocks at the worst possible time each year, you'd still have $228,000, almost $60,000 more than if you bought bonds instead. The moral is that the more risk you are willing to assume and the more of your portfolio you invest in stocks, the more wealth you will generate. The way you split up your money between stocks and bonds depends primarily on your risk aversion.

Analyzing Your Own Risk Aversion

In analyzing how much of your portfolio you are willing to invest in stocks, don't fall victim to the traditional formulas offered in all those well-meaning publications at the newsstand. Pick up any investment magazine and you'll probably find an article that offers advice on how someone of a particular age should balance her portfolio. It might say something like "A thirty-year-old should put 80 percent of her investment dollars in stocks, while a sixty-year-old should only have 20 percent of her money in stocks."

Such formulas work only when based on all those assumptions—you'd help your parents pay for their elder care, you'd pay for your child's college education, and most of all, you want to retire at age sixty-five and maintain your current life-style—I've suggested you abandon in order to survive the squeeze. Without those assumptions the choices truly become individual. So how much risk should you assume?

The answer, I believe, is to look at your chances to recoup losses. The younger you are and the longer you intend to work, the more opportunities you'll have to recover from financial loss. If you're a baby boomer and you're following my program for surviving the squeeze, you're going to have a great many years to recover from any short-term losses in the stock market. On average, you'll be living to age eighty-five. And since you're not going to retire at sixty-five, you'll be working as long as you're able. I can't make this judgment for you; you'll have to do it on your own. As for myself, I'm sixty-four years old, and my income-supplement fund is entirely invested in stocks.

It's important to realize that there are other ways you can minimize the risk of investing in stocks other than balancing your portfolio: you can invest in a wide variety of companies by purchasing a mutual fund; and you can practice dollar/cost averaging.

218

The Dangers of Stock Picking

The stock market used to be considered very risky for the average investor. That was because if you had only a small amount of money you could only buy a small number of different stocks. You were forced to pick out a handful of individual stocks and pin your future to the fates of those few companies. This practice, called stock picking, is extremely risky. Only a genius who's also able to see into the future can succeed at it. That's because the financial health of even the biggest companies is nearly impossible to predict.

I asked Tom Rodman of the investment banking firm of Alex Brown & Sons, Inc., to help me come up with evidence of how risky stock picking is. First, Tom went back and charted how three computer companies, which were very popular with stock pickers, have actually fared over the last several years.

	High	Today	% Change
International Business Machines (IBM)	175	48	down 72
Digital Equipment (DEC)	199.5	40	down 80
Apple Computer (AAPL)	73.25	38	down 48

Then I asked Tom to calculate how some individual stocks that were popular with stock pickers have fared in the past eighteen months:

	Year High	Today	% Change
Merck & Co. (MRK)	53 $^3/_8$	34 $^1/_2$	down 35
Phillip Morris (MO)	86 $^5/_8$	49 $^1/_2$	down 42
U.S. Surgical (USS)	106 $^7/_8$	27 $^5/_8$	down 74
Amgen (AMGN)	78	35 $^1/_2$	down 54

As you can see, if you had relied on just a handful of such "sure things," your investment would have lost a great deal of its value.

Wealthy individuals have always been able to mitigate the effects that such falls in value of particular stocks have on their total portfolio by investing in a great number of different companies. The rich were able to spread their sizable investments among different companies and industries and thereby take advantage of the overall upward trend of the stock market. A fairly recent innovation, called the mutual fund, has given the average investor the same opportunity.

The Advantages of Mutual Funds

A mutual fund is an investment pool. It takes money from many individual investors, pools it together, and buys a portfolio of common stocks and/or bonds. Those who manage the pool take a portion of the money invested—generally between .25 and 1.5 percent—and apply it to their expenses. They may, or may not, charge an up-front sales commission, called a "load." Funds may also charge fees to cover marketing and advertising and/or fees when you sell shares. These fees reduce the share of each investor's money that is actually invested, not the yield on the investments. That is shared by the members of the pool.

By purchasing a mutual stock fund you can diversify your investments far more than you could on your own. In addition, you're getting full-time professional management of your investment. The track record of that management is the only way to judge a mutual fund. Since you can't see into the future, all you can do is research how the fund did in past years and assume that as long as management remains the same, it will do equally well or poorly in the future. Most of the magazines covering personal finance run annual features rating the thousands of mutual funds on the market.

Mutual Fund Options

Mutual funds have different missions and philosophies that affect their level of risk and perhaps their yield. Here are the major types:

- Balanced funds combine stock investments with bond investments in an effort to minimize the risks inherent in stocks.
- Growth stock funds invest in the stocks of companies, both large and small, that are believed to have the potential for long-term growth.
- Aggressive growth stock funds pursue the same goal as growth funds but take greater risks in an effort to get greater rewards.
- Growth/income stock funds look for stocks that offer both dividends and the potential for long-term growth in value.
- Equity-income stock funds invest primarily in the stocks of well-known companies that pay regular and sizable dividends.
- Index stock funds simply invest their pool of money in all the stocks that make up one of the major stock market indices, such as Standard & Poor's 500.
- Socially responsible stock funds invest their pool of money in companies that match the set of values the particular fund espouses. For instance, the companies may all have good environmental records or treat their employees well.
- Small-company stock funds invest primarily in the stocks of small companies that the fund managers believe will grow over time.
- Sector stock funds invest in the stocks of companies in one particular industry, or sector, of the market.
- International stock funds invest in the stocks of companies from outside the United States.
- Global stock funds invest in the stocks of both foreign and domestic companies.
- Municipal bond funds invest in long and intermediate municipal bonds that offer tax-free income.
- Corporate bond funds invest either wholly or primarily in the bond issues of publicly traded corporations.
- U.S. government income funds invest in treasury bonds, federally guaranteed mortgage-backed securities, and government notes.

- Ginnie Mae funds invest primarily in mortgage securities guaranteed by the Government National Mortgage Association.

Hire a Financial Adviser to Help You Select Mutual Fund Investments

If I've confused you a bit by listing all these types of funds, I'm glad. You see, while mutual funds make investing less risky, that doesn't mean they've made it child's play. Despite all the articles about mutual funds you'll find in the media, I believe you should still enlist the aid of a financial professional to guide you in your investing.

As I mentioned in the previous chapter, I suggest you look for a financial adviser who charges an hourly fee, not a percentage or commission. (For advice on finding and interviewing financial advisers, see page 194.) If you've already lined up a financial adviser to help with either your parent's or child's finances, don't reflexively use her for your own investing. By all means add her to your list of candidates, but interview her just as rigorously. Just because an adviser does a good job with Medicaid planning or with financial aid for college tuition doesn't mean she'll do a good job helping you select mutual funds. In addition to all the other prerequisites for a financial adviser, make sure the individual you select develops a customized plan that matches your needs and wants rather than simply applying some traditional formula to your situation.

The Ultimate Responsibility Is Still Your Own

Even though you'll be sitting down with a carefully selected financial adviser, it doesn't mean you should relinquish control over your own investments. It's your future you're building, and it's ultimately your responsibility. An adviser should do just what the name implies: advise. You are the one who should make the decisions. In order for those decisions to be informed, you need to learn a little bit about how to judge mutual funds.

The only real guide on the future performance of a fund is its past performance. That's indicative of the fund manager's success at putting together a portfolio that performs well. Any change in management may affect a fund's performance. You can get figures on a fund's performance in any of the annual mutual fund surveys conducted by publications such as *Money*, *U.S. News & World Report*, and *Consumer Reports*.

Recent studies seem to indicate that over the long haul most soundly managed funds of similar types perform pretty much the same. The only difference in an investor's yield, therefore, is the amount the fund charges for its services; the less a fund charges, the more an investment yields for the individual investor. That means you should pay special attention to costs, fees, and expenses, which will be outlined in the fund's prospectus under a heading called expense summary. The bottom line of that chart should be a number called expense ratio. That's the total of all expenses expressed as a percentage of total assets. All other things being equal, you should select the fund with the lower expense ratio.

Carefully read the part of the prospectus labeled objectives. This will tell you how the fund tries to make its profits and which of the general types of funds I've outlined above it belongs to. Compare your personal need for growth and your personal aversion to risk to the fund's stated philosophy and approach. Don't buy the fund unless they match.

Finally, read through the entire prospectus carefully, paying particular attention to any sentences in capital letters. That's the way most funds try to identify what are called "special risks."

Dollar/Cost Averaging: Slow and Steady Wins the Race

You can further minimize the risk of investing in stocks by practicing an investment technique called dollar/cost averaging. The idea is to invest the same amount of money at set intervals regardless of how the market is doing at that particular time. By investing the same amount of money rather than trying to buy the same number of shares in a mutual fund or trying to pick the best times to buy, over time you'll actually reduce your average cost per share.

Let's say you decide you can invest $200 each month in a growth stock mutual fund. The first month, shares are priced at $1 each, so you're able to buy 200 shares. The next month shares go up to $2 each, so you're only able to buy 100 shares. In two months you've spent $400 for 300 shares. That's an average price per share of $1.33. If you instead decided to buy 200 shares each month, regardless of price, they would have cost you $200 the first month and $400 the second month, for an average price of $1.50 per share. If you tried to pick your spots, you might have timed it right and bought 400 shares that first month when they were only $1 each. But you also could have timed it poorly and ended up buying 400 shares when they were $2 each. In other words, timed buying is a gamble. The more frequently you invest, the more effective your dollar/cost averaging.

Your Investment Program

Let me pull all these elements together and outline my advice about investing for your future.

1. Dedicate as much as you can each month out of your stream of income for an income-supplement fund.
2. Analyze your own risk aversion and determine about how much you need to balance the risk of investing in stocks by also investing in bonds.
3. Sit down with a financial adviser and examine which mutual funds appear to match your needs and wants.
4. Research the past history of any mutual fund you're thinking of buying and also read its prospectus carefully.
5. Practice dollar/cost averaging by buying the same number of mutual fund shares each month regardless of market conditions.

One further word of advice: Remember, you're investing for the long term, not the short term. Don't become obsessive and constantly measure the performance of your portfolio. Of course, if there are any major changes in your life that affect your finances, make sure to speak to your adviser about them. Barring such changes, once your investment program is up and running, you can relax and simply schedule an annual checkup with your adviser to review everything. You'll have done all that you could. The rest is up to time.

What Will the Future Be Like?

What will the world look like when you start having to draw on this income-supplement fund? Despite the current doom and gloom, I think it will be a lot better than most people think, globally, politically, and personally.

Globally

America, which today seems ready to fall behind the European Community and Japan economically, will probably be in much better shape than either of those economic competitors. That's because the populations of Europe and Japan are much older than America's and have lower birthrates. In addition, America has always been a heterogeneous society open to immigrants—another source of youth, enthusiasm, and energy—while Europe and Japan are homogeneous societies closed to most immigrants. Therefore, while our society may be aging, it will still be younger than our major competitors.

Politically

The current trend of government spending a disproportionately greater amount of money on the old than on the young will be reversed. Boomers, who are just now learning to flex their political muscle as a group, will be firmly in charge. Sure, some of

225

those societal advantages their aging parents fought so hard to hold on to will look quite appealing. But since boomers had children later in life, their kids will still be in, or at least hovering around, the parental nest. And since boomers may not have been able to do everything they would have liked for their kids, they'll look to government to fill the gap.

Personally

Ironically, I think those who follow the program outlined in this book and resolve to live for today will actually have brighter tomorrows. They'll have abandoned get-rich-quick approaches and conspicuous consumption and will be prudent investors and savvy consumers. They'll be living long, productive lives, working at careers they find rewarding for as long as they possibly can. They'll have empowered their parents to "not go gentle into that good night" and to take charge of the rest of their lives. And they'll pass on to their children one of life's great lessons—success is doing the best you can with what you've got.

While my crystal ball is no clearer than yours, I can tell you that those of my baby boomer clients who have implemented the seven steps I've outlined in this book are happier and less fearful of the future than they were before. Take Sydney and Lucy Carton, for example.

If you recall from chapter 1, Sydney is a forty-five-year-old account executive at an advertising agency and Lucy is a forty-three-year-old magazine editor. They have an eight-year-old daughter named Brittany. When they first came to see me, they were embarrassed that they had no retirement savings, were afraid Lucy's aging mother might need their financial help, were frightened they wouldn't be able to pay for their daughter's education, and were worried Lucy might lose her job.

Since then, Sydney has secured his position in the agency but has started to expand his network. Lucy launched a preemptive strike, found out that layoffs were indeed in the works, and was able to negotiate her way into an at-home, independent contractor's position with the magazine. While she lost her benefits, she's still covered by Sydney's. And she has been able to line up other magazine clients.

By paying attention to every penny they spend and trimming back their life insurance coverage, Sydney and Lucy were able to come up with enough money to establish an emergency cash reserve and to take out two disability insurance policies.

They both sat down with Lucy's mother, had a long talk about what they could and couldn't do for her, and then helped her find a good-quality long-term-care insurance policy. And while Sydney still sometimes dreams of sending Brittany to Princeton, he and Lucy are concentrating on teaching her how to take charge of her own financial life (although at the moment that consists primarily of selecting which Barney puppet to buy).

And as I finish writing this book, Sydney and Lucy are in the process of going over their mutual fund options with a financial planner I recommended.

Their futures are bright—and so is yours.

Index

Index

Index

Index

Index